FRESHWATER AQUARIUM CARE

A Comprehensive Guide for Tropical Fish Hobbyists

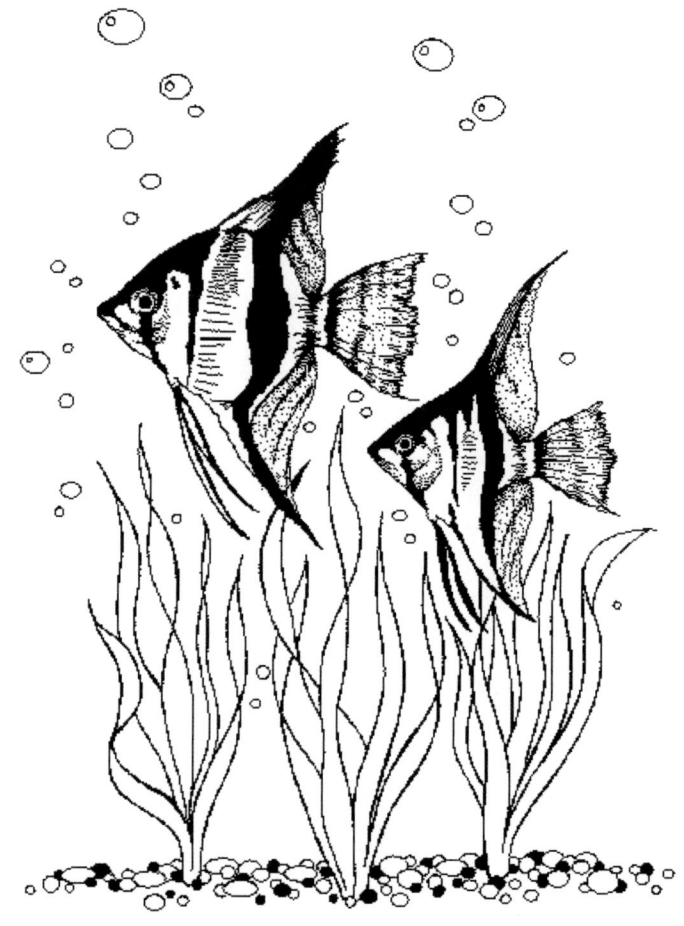

Kevin J. Ruff, PhD.

Freshwater Aquarium Chemistry: A Comprehensive Guide for Tropical Fish Hobbyists

by Kevin J. Ruff, Ph.D.

Copyright © 2009 AquaChem Publishing

ISBN 978-0-9841216-1-8

www.AquaChemPublishing.com

All rights reserved. No part of this publication may be reproduced, stored in a retrieval system, or transmitted in any form or by any means, electronic, mechanical, photocopying, recording, scanning, or otherwise, without the prior written permission of the Publisher.

LIMIT OF LIABILITY/DISCLAIMER OF WARRANTY: THE PUBLISHER AND THE AUTHOR MAKE NO REPRESENTATIONS OR WARRANTIES WITH RESPECT TO THE ACCURACY OR COMPLETENESS OF THE CONTENTS OF THIS WORK AND SPECIFICALLY DISCLAIM ALL WARRANTIES, INCLUDING WITHOUT LIMITATION WARRANTIES OF FITNESS FOR A PARTICULAR PURPOSE. NEITHER THE PUBLISHER NOR THE AUTHOR SHALL BE LIABLE FOR DAMAGES ARISING HEREFROM.

PREFACE

For most people, the thought of an aquarium conjures up visions of beautiful fish elegantly swimming through crystal clear water. But, for some this vision suddenly **mutates** to one of horror -- one of expensive, bloated fish floating throughout the now murky water that once filled their beautifully decorated aquarium. The sad fact of the matter is that the proper maintenance of your aquarium is necessary to avert a heartrending "ending" like the one just described. No one wants their venture into a new hobby to end in disaster, as they watch both money and fish go down the drain. This situation ultimately leaves you with only two options: **1) leave the hobby** or **2) make a trip to the nearest bookstore or pet shop** to gain the know-how you need to avert a second, third, or fourth disaster. Unfortunately, many beginners choose option one -- sometimes, never to return. Those diehard hobbyists who do choose option two usually find just enough information in the available books to prevent a continuous disaster, but the occasional semi-disaster continues to plague them. They eventually find their way to a book like this one. The sudden and usually unexplained loss of some or all of your beautiful pets is one of the unfortunate occurrences that detracts from the enjoyment of keeping and breeding tropical fish. More often than not, the loss is due to poor "water quality".

"Water quality" is a subjective term and with it comes inherent problems. One species' poor water quality can be another species' heaven. Aquarists need to know as much as possible about each species they will keep. Without this knowledge, this book or any other advice about water quality would be hit-or-miss.

Understanding the chemistry of your freshwater aquarium is hard enough conceptually without having to wade through the technical jargon

Find Related Information at: www.AquaChemPublishing.com

of chemists. Unfortunately, as with other subjects (i.e. computers, medicine, etc.), it's difficult, if not impossible, to discuss and explain the concepts without a common vocabulary. I've tried to limit my use of technical terms as much as possible. Those terms which I just couldn't do without, I've explained further in a sidebar in the margin of the page containing the term in question. Terms included in sidebars are indicated with **bold italics** throughout the book. An example is shown in the left margin.

pH : a measure of the acidity of water.

I'd like to thank all those who have contributed to my knowledge of chemistry and tropical fish. I'd especially like to thank Eric L. Taylor for proofreading my book before it went to press.

Kevin J. Ruff

Find Related Information at: www.AquaChemPublishing.com

Table of Contents

	Page
Preface	iii

Chapter 1: The Nature of Water

Water's Structure	1
What Makes Water A Liquid?	2
Solubility – What dissolves & why?	3
Heat Capacity – Use of aquarium heaters.	5
Properties of Municipal Water	7
Dechlorination	9
Chloramine Removal	10
Properties of Natural Water	11
Water & The Natural Environment	13
Chapter At-A-Glance	15

Chapter 2: pH - The Chemical pHacts

So What Is pH?	18
What Affects pH?	20
Signs & Symptoms of pH Problems	21
Testing pH	24
Correcting pH Mayhem	25
One Final pHact	32
Chapter At-A-Glance	33

Chapter 3: Water Hardness

Lessening The Confusion	35
What Makes Water Hard?	36
The Water Hardness Vocabulary	38

Find Related Information at: www.AquaChemPublishing.com

Signs & Symptoms of Hardness Problems 40
Testing Water Hardness 44
Softening Hard Water 45
Chapter At-A-Glance 48

Chapter 4: The Nitrogen Cycle

The Making of A Cycle 49
Diagram of A Cycle 51
Signs & Symptoms of A Broken Cycle 54
Testing Ammonia 54
Correcting Ammonia Mayhem 56
Testing Nitrites 57
Correcting Nitrite Mayhem 58
Testing Nitrates 58
Correcting Nitrate Mayhem 59
Chapter At-A-Glance 61

Chapter 5: Aquarium Setup & Maintenance

Initial Setup 65
    Location: 66
    Filtration: 66
    Vegetation: 68
    Speciation: 68
Conditioning an Aquarium 69
Aquarium Maintenance 74

Index 79

Find Related Information at: www.AquaChemPublishing.com

Chapter 1: *The Nature of Water*

The Nature of Water

ater is one of the most chemically unique substances on earth and understanding its "nature" is of utmost importance to anyone seriously considering keeping tropical fish. Fish can't live without water and if an aquarist isn't careful fish can't live with it either. Anyone who has put too many fish in an aquarium that couldn't support them will agree that the sudden, unexplained loss of a tank-full of tropical fish is money (& dead fish) down the drain. More often than not, this unfortunate occurrence is due to the aquarist's ignorance of the nature of water. So just what is the nature of water?

Water's Structure

Water is comprised of two hydrogen atoms and one oxygen atom (written in chemistry shorthand as H_2O). Due to the greatly differing **electronegativities** of hydrogen and oxygen, water is very polar. This polarity leads to a partial negative charge (δ-) on the oxygen atom and a partial positive charge (δ+) on each hydrogen atom (See **Figure 1-1**). The polarity of water, in one way or another, leads to all of its unique properties.

electronegativity: the pulling force an atom has on its electrons. The stronger the force, the more electronegative an atom is.

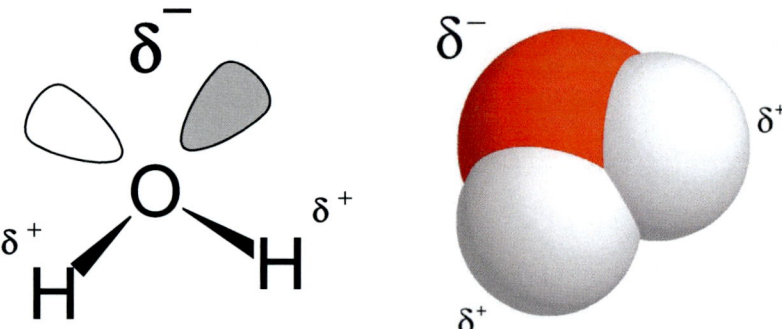

Figure 1-1: (Left) A representation of water showing the orbitals that contain the unshared pairs of electrons on the central oxygen atom and the partial charges (δ^- & δ^+) on the respective atoms. (Right) A space filling model of water showing the relative sizes of the participating atoms as well as the partial charges associated with each atom.

What Makes Water A Liquid?

The first striking property of water is the fact that it is a high boiling liquid. Room temperature is around 24°C or ~75°F and water boils at 100°C or 212°F. Hydrogen sulfide (H_2S in chemistry shorthand), an ***analog*** of water, has a molecular weight that is almost double that of water, but is nevertheless a gas at room temperature. Not only is hydrogen sulfide a gas, but it is also extremely foul-smelling (it's the smell from rotten eggs) and toxic to humans. I'm sure that everyone's glad that water is neither toxic nor smelly. Water is a liquid as a result of ***hydrogen bonding*** between water molecules. And, ***hydrogen bonds*** are a direct result of water's polarity. Partially positive hydrogen atoms on one molecule of water interact with partially negative oxygen atoms of other molecules of water. This results in a highly ordered lattice-like structure. In order for water to boil, this ordered system of hydrogen bonds must be destroyed, and that requires energy. And so, water boils much higher than compounds of similar molecular structure or weight.

analog: a series of compounds that are similar in composition and structure. These similarities are supposed to result in the related com-pounds having similar chemical properties.

hydrogen bond: a weak attractive force between hydrogen atoms that are bound to highly electronegative atoms (oxygen, nitrogen, etc.) and unshared pairs of electrons on similar atoms of other molecules.

Find Related Information at: www.AquaChemPublishing.com

Chapter 1: *The Nature of Water*

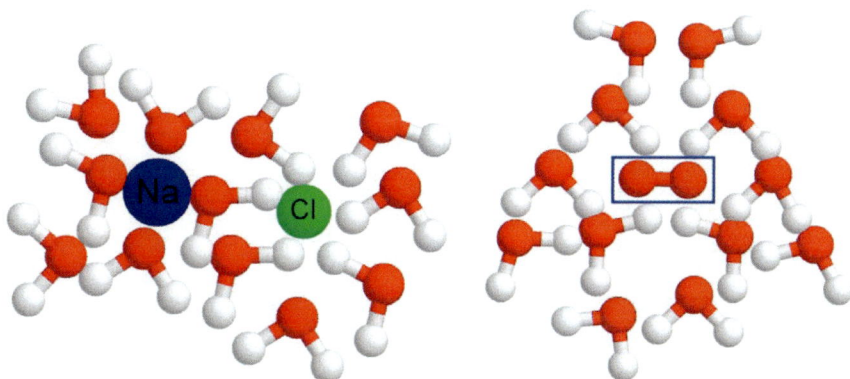

Figure 1-2: (Left) A representation of the solvation of sodium (Na^{1+}) and chloride (Cl^{1-}) ions from a molecule of table salt. (Right) A representation of a dissolved molecule of oxygen (O_2). A rectangle has been placed around the oxygen molecule to help locate it.

Solubility – What dissolves & why?

Water is known as the universal solvent. Most common salts will dissolve in it, as well as many organic compounds. And, luckily for fish, so will gases -- including all-important oxygen (O_2 in chemistry shorthand).

Salts, like table salt and baking soda, are *ionic* compounds and are soluble in water because of its high polarity. The positively or negatively charged *ion* interacts with the opposite partial charge on water molecules (see **Figure 1-2**). The solvation of *ionic* compounds actually increases the order of the lattice-like structure described previously. As a result, it requires more energy to effect a change in the water's temperature (warming or cooling). This is why saltwater boils at a higher temperature and freezes at a lower temperature. People take advantage of this effect when making homemade ice cream or when they sprinkle rock salt on a frozen sidewalk.

ion: an atom that has gained or lost electrons and, as a result, is charged. i.e. NaCl (table salt) in water exists as Na^{1+} and Cl^{1-}.

Find Related Information at: www.AquaChemPublishing.com

Organic compounds, such as sugar and drinking alcohol, that have enough groups capable of **hydrogen bonding** with water are also soluble in it. Organic amines that result from decaying plants or animals are also water soluble. They generally impart a yellow-brown tint to the water as well as an unpleasant odor.

Likewise, gases like oxygen, that are capable of **hydrogen bonding** with water, will dissolve in it (see **Figure 1-2**). The solubility of oxygen in water is of great importance to aquarists -- and even more so to their tropical fish. Oxygen is more soluble in cold water than it is in warm (so is carbon dioxide). However, most species of tropical fish can't tolerate cold water. Their metabolism slows, they become lethargic, and eventually they die. So, obviously cooling your aquarium is not the answer. Gas solubility is also heavily dependent upon the access of the gases to the water. What this means is that the surface area of the water is extremely important for the gases to be able to exchange. If you measured the oxygen content in two aquaria of equal volume but with widely differing dimensions (see **Figure 1-3**), you would find that the aquarium with the larger surface area would by far have the highest oxygen level. Both oxygen and carbon dioxide (CO_2 in chemistry shorthand) will exchange more rapidly in an aquarium with a larger surface area. This fact has to be considered when stocking an aquarium. If there is not enough dissolved oxygen for all of the fish, the less hardy or weaker fish will die until a livable oxygen level is reached that will meet the oxygen demand.

Chapter 1: *The Nature of Water*

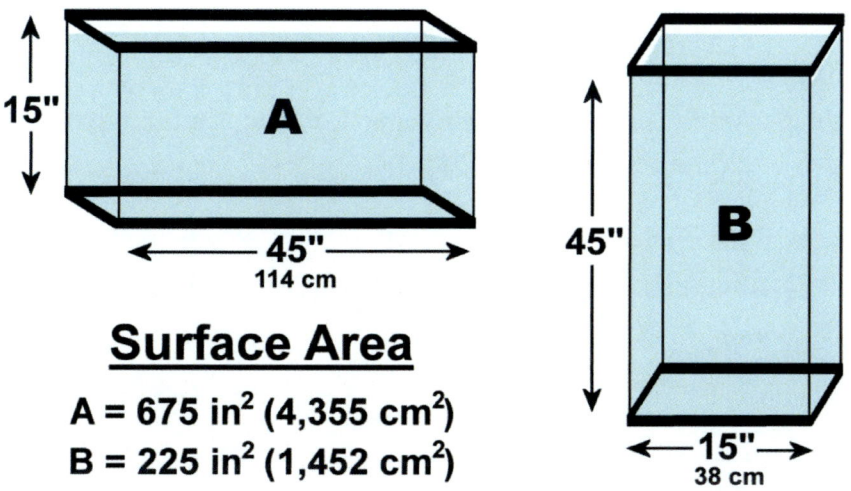

Figure 1-3: An exaggerated example of two aquaria with equal volumes but with greatly differing surface areas.

One way to raise an aquarium's ability to support more fish is by the use of an aerator. Air stones, most types of filters, or anything else that will disturb the water's surface will greatly enhance the rate of exchange for gases. This allows aquarists to keep many more fish in an aquarium that would otherwise not support them. Aeration has also made it possible to make aquaria in shapes that have very little surface area. One area on which this has had an impact is interior design. It's often preferable, from an artistic perspective, for a designer to use tall cylindrical aquaria as decorative columns in a hallway despite the biological dilemma of oxygen exchange.

Heat Capacity – Use of aquarium heaters.

A much lesser known, yet important property of water is its high heat capacity. Heat capacity is a substance's ability to absorb heat energy without changing temperature. Heat capacity is why a watched pot never seems to boil. It takes a huge amount of energy to heat water to its boiling point. Just as water can absorb a lot of energy without warming, it can also lose a lot of energy without cooling. As a result, lakes don't warm too much in the daytime or cool too much at night. This provides cold blooded creatures like fish with a temperately stable environment. Right now you're probably thinking, "Heat capacity's interesting, and I'm glad you've explained why fish survive in the wild, but how does this affect my aquarium?"

An aquarium is exposed to the environment on all sides. So it gains or loses heat much more rapidly than would a lake. An aquarium placed too near a window by an unaware aquarist can quickly overheat in the summertime. That same aquarium in the wintertime will also become dangerously cold for tropical fish very quickly. The obvious solution to avoid this extreme variation in temperature is not to place your aquarium too near a window. That not withstanding, most people don't maintain their home at tropical climate temperatures (~27°C or ~80°F), at least not year-round. To alleviate this problem an aquarist can purchase an aquarium heater. These helpful devices have a thermostat that turns on their heating coils whenever the aquarium water needs warming. Like light bulbs, aquarium heaters are rated in Watts. If the temperature of the room where you want to keep your aquarium is close to the desired aquarium temperature, you will not need a high Wattage heater. For most smaller aquaria (less than 35 gallons) a heater rating of 2-3 Watts per gallon will be sufficient. If you have a larger aquarium, it's recommended that you use two heaters 4-5 Watts per gallon placed at opposite ends of the aquarium. This will greatly lessen

Chapter 1: *The Nature of Water*

temperature variations throughout the aquarium that could create stress for sensitive species of fish. As an added benefit, if one heater fails the aquarium will not be completely without heat. Hopefully, this way your fish will survive until you can replace the bad heater.

One very common mistake that new aquarists make when setting up their first aquarium is to turn the heater up too high too quickly. They don't realize just how long it takes to change the temperature of their aquarium water. Ideally, you will set up your aquarium and get the water equilibrated long before you add any fish. If you don't you may end up with parboiled fish. Realistically, though, you should always adjust your heater dial very slightly over long periods of time to allow the water temperature to re-equilibrate.

Properties of Municipal Water

Over the course of time, most hobbyists will use municipal tap water to fill or refill their aquaria. One of the great nuisances of doing this is that this water usually contains chlorine or chloramine. Chlorine and/or chloramine are used to destroy waterborne pathogens such as coliform bacteria (*E. coli*), cholera, or cryptosporidium. One or two **parts per million** (ppm) of these disinfectants are usually added to water supplies at the local water treatment plant and **must** be removed before being used in an aquarium. Unfortunately, your local municipality can't provide you with water that's both safe to drink and safe for tropical fish.

Chlorine and chloramine are both strong oxidizing agents. They will quickly damage the gill tissues of fish. Chlorine (Cl_2 in chemistry shorthand) does this mainly through the generation of hypochlorite ions (ClO^{1-} in chemistry shorthand) when it is added to

parts per million (ppm): one part of compound in question in one million parts of solvent. This is equivalent to milligrams per liter ($^{mg}/_L$).

Find Related Information at: www.AquaChemPublishing.com

water (see **Figure 1-4**). Hypochlorite is the active ingredient in household bleach. NEVER clean an aquarium with bleach water. There is usually at least 5% hypochlorite in bleach and it will be left behind after the water evaporates. Bleach is usually diluted 1 cup (~250 milliliters) per gallon (~3.8 liters) or less. This leads to a hypochlorite concentration of more than 3000 *ppm*. Even if the bleach was used 100 times more dilute than normal, there would still be more than 30 *ppm* of hypochlorite. This concentration would easily destroy an entire aquarium of fish. Not only would the bleach kill the fish, it would also destroy all biological filtration and that would also likely lead to fish death.

equilibrium: a state in which product formation and reversal to reactants or starting compounds is in balance. An example is that of a bath tub that's being filled while the drain is open. As long as the water pouring in is equal to the water draining out, the water in the bath tub is in a state of equilibrium.

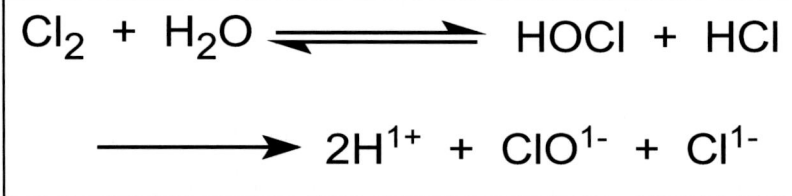

Figure 1-4: Equilibrium of chlorine (Cl_2) dissolved in water. Note that two molecules of acid are produced. This is of little concern as this occurs in parts per million.

The use of chloramine has become much more common in recent years. One reason for this is that chlorine is a gas and slowly dissipates from water over time. People living further from the water treatment plant usually have a lower chlorine concentration than those living nearby. Also, when chlorine reacts with dissolved organics, it can eventually form chloroform, and chloroform has been indicated as a probable carcinogen. Chloramine is produced when chlorine reacts with ammonia. Once it has reacted with ammonia, it will no longer react with dissolved organics, but it **is** still a very effective disinfectant.

Chapter 1: *The Nature of Water*

Dechlorination

There are several ways to remove chlorine from tap water. One is by simple diffusion. Chlorine is a gas and will diffuse from water if given enough time or if assisted by surface agitation. You can either allow your water to stand for several days or you can place an air stone in the bucket of water overnight.

Another way to remove chlorine is to pass the water through high quality, unused activated carbon several times. While the immediacy of this method is acceptable, it's not very economical. For all practical purposes, this is an outdated technique.

If you want to dechlorinate quickly and economically, you should use a dechlorinating agent. Chlorine and hypochlorite can both be neutralized by sodium thiosulfate ($Na_2S_2O_3$ in chemistry shorthand). This is the active ingredient in most aquarium water dechlorinating agents. The neutralization is almost instantaneous so the water can be used immediately. Two molecules of thiosulfate will reduce one molecule of chlorine or two molecules of hypochlorite (see **Figure 1-5**). Dechlorinators are usually a 1% solution of sodium thiosulfate, so 1 drop per gallon of this solution will remove approximately 5 *ppm* of chlorine. This excess ensures that all of the disinfectant will be neutralized. You may want to use slightly more if you are setting up a brand new aquarium and will be adding fish immediately.

Find Related Information at: www.AquaChemPublishing.com

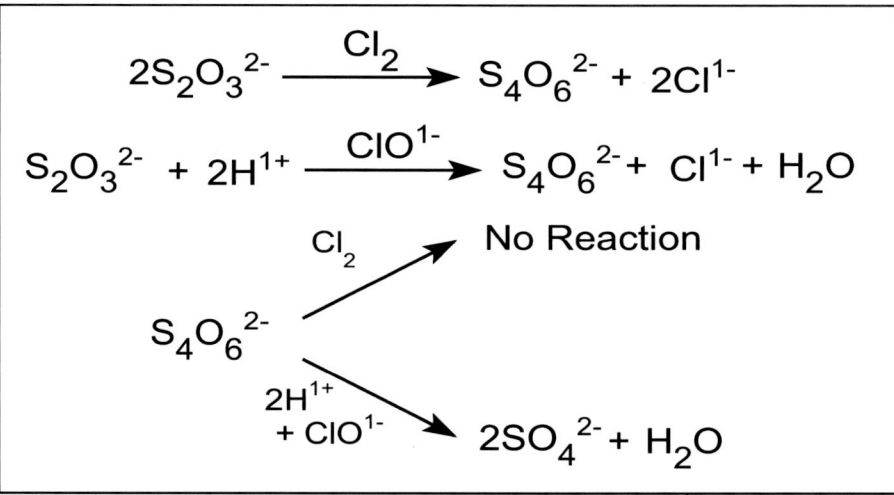

Figure 1-5: Reactions of chlorine (Cl_2) & hypochlorite ion (ClO^{1-}) with thiosulfate ion ($S_2O_3^{2-}$) & subsequently tetrathionate ion ($S_4O_6^{2-}$).

Chloramine Removal

Chloramine, like chlorine, can also be broken down by sodium thiosulfate. Unfortunately, when this occurs free ammonia equivalent to the initial concentration of the chloramine, is generated. Depending on the amount of water being treated this may or may not be a problem. That is, if you are performing a small partial water change (less than 25%) and have well established biological filtration, the 1 *ppm* or so of free ammonia will be diluted immediately to 0.25 *ppm* or less and will be removed by biological filtration in a very short time. If you are performing a larger partial water change or have the need to introduce fish immediately, chloramine would present an extreme problem.

One solution is to remove the free ammonia with either naturally occurring zeolite chips or synthetic molecular sieves (see **Chapter 4** for more on ammonia and the nitrogen cycle). Ammonia removal is a very slow process.

parts per million (ppm): one part of compound in question in one million parts of solvent. This is equivalent to milligrams per liter ($^{mg}/_L$).

Chapter 1: *The Nature of Water*

Fortunately, unique aquarium products exist that can not only break down chloramine, but also instantaneously react with the newly freed ammonia. The harmless reaction byproducts are then acted upon by the biological filter.

One of these products is chemically known as sodium hydroxymethanesulfonate and is sold by Kordon under the trade name AmQuel®. It's also sold by Tetra under the trade name AquaSafe®. This product is purported by its makers to remain active in the aquarium for ammonia scavenging unless removed by activated carbon or by water changes.

Another of these products is sold by Aquarium Pharmaceuticals under the trade name Ammo-Lock 2®. These products provide both fish suppliers and hobbyists with a fast and convenient way to generate safe aquarium water.

Properties of Natural Water

Many hobbyists will also use natural water sources to fill or refill their aquaria. The primary natural water used by aquarists is that of well water. Most wells are drilled fairly deep to prevent contamination by surface water that may contain pathogens picked up from farm animal feces or insecticides picked up from a nearby crop field. In most parts of the United States, water filters through geological formations, such as limestone, on its journey to the earth's water table. During this trip the water absorbs inorganic salts from these geological formations. The main **cations** acquired on the trip are: calcium, magnesium, iron, and some aluminum. The main **anions** acquired are: carbonate, sulfate, and some nitrate. Depending on the geology of the region where you live, your well

cation: (kat-ion) a positively charged ion.

anion: (ann-ion) a negatively charged ion.

Find Related Information at: www.AquaChemPublishing.com

water can have a water hardness rating anywhere from soft to extremely hard (see **Chapter 3** for more on water hardness). Hard water can lead to problems with sensitive species of fish. It can result in quite an alkaline pH from dissolved carbonate salts (see **Chapter 2** for more on pH) which can, in turn, make the effects of ammonia toxicity more pronounced (see **Chapter 4** for more on ammonia).

Your aquarium water's hardness may not be of extreme concern initially, but over time salts will slowly concentrate. Even with partial water changes, this still occurs because the well water is not free of salts. The harder your well water, the more rapidly this concentration phenomenon will occur. Eventually, even with hardier species of fish, this will have a detrimental effect.

There are many methods for reducing water hardness and/or removing *ions*. One simple and fairly inexpensive way is to perform small partial water changes (less than 20%) with distilled water. Another way is to employ some sort of water softener. These softeners usually work in conjunction with normal filtration and can be reused after recharging in a concentrated table salt (NaCl in chemistry shorthand) solution. Yet another way is to purchase a water filtration system such as a ***reverse osmosis*** system. These systems are fairly expensive and require regular maintenance.

If you intend to use well water for your aquarium, be sure to test it thoroughly before introducing any fish. And remember, since your water doesn't come from a municipality, you won't have to worry about chlorine or chloramine removal.

osmosis: the flow of water through a semi-permeable membrane (one that will allow water to pass, but not ions) from an area of high water concentration to an area of low water concentration.

reverse osmosis: using a pump to force water to flow in reverse, that is from an area of low water concentration to an area of high water concentration.

Chapter 1: *The Nature of Water*

Water & The Natural Environment

Because of the many factors influencing it, water chemistry is quite complicated. However, as with most things, nature has made it so that all things will remain in a delicate balance if left undisturbed. The problem is that, as aquarists, we try to take only a portion of the natural environment and put it in an aquarium. This ruins the balance of the water chemistry and, as would follow logically, problems arise. So, if we can mimic nature as much as possible in our aquaria, they will require very little maintenance.

One of the unavoidable maintenance jobs would be to periodically add water to replace the water that has evaporated. Nature does this every time it rains substantially. Rain is pure water except for man-made contaminants like air pollutants that are picked up as the rain drops fall from the sky. So, it only makes sense to add pure water to an aquarium if all you're doing is replacing evaporated water. This helps to slow the concentrating of water soluble compounds that occurs over time, and it mimics nature. Distilled water can be purchased at grocery or discount stores for water replacement. **Note:** Do not confuse water <u>replacement</u> with water <u>changes</u>. They are two completely different things. A water change is when you remove a portion (usually 25-50%) of the water in the aquarium and add fresh water to replace it. You are exchanging water to remove the water soluble compounds mentioned earlier that are concentrating. Water changes can be done with distilled water as long as it's no more than ~10-20% at one time. Any more than this may cause undue stress for the aquarium inhabitants, especially for sensitive species. It's possible to avoid water changes if you: 1) don't overcrowd your aquarium, 2) you keep it well planted with hardy plants, and 3) perform water replacement with distilled water. Remember, if you make an effort to create as natural an environment as possible, it will require much less effort to maintain your aquarium. This saves both money and time.

A planted aquarium filled with livebearing Red Wagtail Platies (*Xiphophorus maculates*).

Chapter 1: *The Nature of Water*

Chapter At-A-Glance

- Water is polar due to electronegativity.
    - Water hydrogen bonds due to its polarity &, as a result, is a liquid.
    - Things like oxygen, ammonia, & inorganic salts are soluble in water because of hydrogen bonding & polarity.
    - Oxygen & carbon dioxide solubility are directly related to aquarium surface area.

- Water has a high heat capacity, so it takes a lot of energy over time to change its temperature.
    - Adjust the aquarium heater only slightly over long periods of time to allow for the temperature to equilibrate.

- Use sodium thiosulfate to destroy chlorine & chloramine found in municipal water. Be aware that destroying chloramine will produce free ammonia.

- Well water can be extremely hard & may need to be softened before it can be used in an aquarium.

- Mimic nature as much as possible to minimize problems in your aquarium environment.
    - Use distilled water for the replacement of evaporated aquarium water.
    - Use distilled water for small (~10-20%) water changes.

Find Related Information at: www.AquaChemPublishing.com

Veiltailed Goldfish (*Carassius auratus*) are not well-suited to a community aquarium, but they can be kept with other goldfish quite readily.

Discus (*Discus rotundatus*) come in many beautiful varieties, but are quite shy fish that require a very large aquarium and require specific water conditions and so can be difficult to keep. Because of this, Discus are not well-suited for a community aquarium.

Find Related Information at: www.AquaChemPublishing.com

Chapter 2: *pH - The Chemical pHacts*

pH - The Chemical pHacts

he first pHact that most hobbyists learn (usually the hard way) is that water quality is the key to success for a freshwater aquarium. And, with a little time and experience, they also learn that pH is both the most useful and convenient indicator of that elusive water quality. All water chemistry affects and is affected by pH in some way.

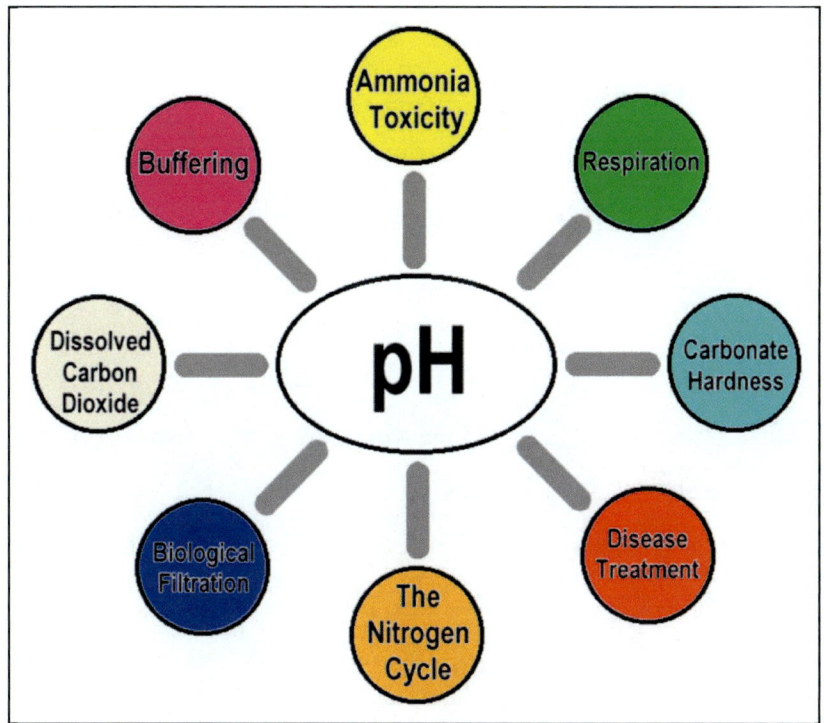

Find Related Information at: www.AquaChemPublishing.com

Ammonia is less toxic to fish at lower pH's. Water that's more acidic (has a low pH) will dissolve more carbonate salts, resulting in harder water. Harder water will lead to a greater **buffering capacity** which will, in turn, have a dominating effect on pH. Since carbon dioxide is part of the carbonate *equilibria*, it's also affected by pH. The nitrogen cycle is perpetually lowering pH (bacterial respiration). As a result, if pH becomes too low, biological filtration will slow. Denitrification during plant or algal photosynthesis raises pH. pH can affect the activity of some disease treatments, as well. For example, low pH inhibits the activity of acriflavines, used for the treatment of external protozoan infections. Conversely, low pH increases the activity of permanganate. Permanganate is used to destroy dissolved organics that can be a source of nutrients for disease causing bacteria. The list goes on and on. pH is truly the center of the aquatic universe.

buffering capacity: buffering is the resistance of water to a change in pH. Its capacity is based on the number of moles of acid or base required to effect a one unit change in pH.

equilibrium: a state in which product formation and reversal to reactants or starting compounds is in balance. An example is that of a bath tub that's being filled while the drain is open. As long as the water pouring in is equal to the water draining out, the water in the bath tub is in a state of equilibrium.

ion: an atom that has gained or lost electrons and, as a result, is charged. i.e. NaCl (table salt) in water exists as Na^{1+} and Cl^{1-}.

So What Is pH?

In a practical sense, pH can be thought of as the measure of acidity or alkalinity of a solution. It's based on a scale from 0 (zero, most acidic) to 14 (most alkaline), however the acceptable pH range for aquarium water is much more limited (see **Figure 2-1**). Acidity or alkalinity of water arises from its ability to form *ions*. When water *ionizes*, it forms hydrogen *ions* (H^{1+}), sometimes referred to as hydronium *ions* (H_3O^{1+}), and hydroxyl *ions* (OH^{1-}) (see **Figure 2-2**). And, pH is a measure of the concentration of the hydrogen *ions* present, properly expressed as: $pH = -\log_{10}[H^{1+}]$, or $pH = -\log_{10}[H_3O^{1+}]$. The [ ] symbols are chemistry shorthand for

Chapter 2: *pH - The Chemical pHacts*

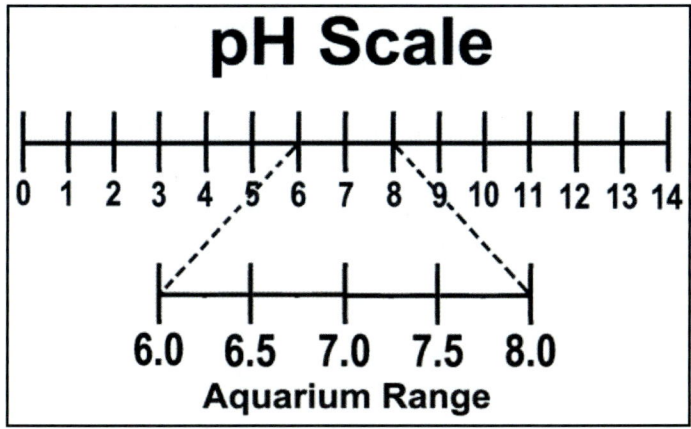

Figure 2-1: The scale for pH with an exploded view of the range for aquarium water.

"concentration" and this concentration is scientifically calculated in a term known as ***moles*** per liter ($^{mol}/_L$) or ***molarity*** (abbreviated "M"). This is of little concern to aquarists, though. ***Molarity*** is just one of many ways to express concentration. You don't have to know what a chemical "***mole***" is or understand ***molarity*** to be able to work with pH as it relates to aquarium water. (If you would like to know more about these terms, they're explained further, in the margin.) The term K_w in **Figure 2-2** is water's ***equilibrium*** constant and is the amount to which the two ***ions*** form. Since there are only

$$H_2O \xrightleftharpoons{K_w = 1 \times 10^{-14}} H^{1+} + OH^{1-}$$

OR

$$2H_2O \xrightleftharpoons{K_w = 1 \times 10^{-14}} H_3O^{1+} + OH^{1-}$$

Figure 2-2: Two alternate ways to express the equilibrium of water ionization at 25°C.

Find Related Information at: www.AquaChemPublishing.com

mole: a mole is 6.022 X 10^{23} atoms or molecules of a substance. That's 6022 followed by 20 zeros. (A billion is only 9 zeros.) The number of molecules in a mole is the same for any element or compound that exists. Due to the differences in the masses of the atoms which comprise a substance, a mole of water (18.02 grams /mole) weighs quite a bit less than a mole of table salt (58.45 grams/mole).

molarity: molarity is simply a mole per liter. Since chemists can't measure a mole, they just weigh out compounds and convert that number into moles.

ion: an atom that has gained or lost electrons and, as a result, is charged. i.e. NaCl (table salt) in water exists as Na^{1+} and Cl^{1-}.

two ions, each ion is formed in 1×10^{-7} mol/L; $(1 \times 10^{-7}) \times (1 \times 10^{-7}) = 1 \times 10^{-14}$. If you have a calculator that can perform base 10 logarithms, you can place 0.0000001 (or 1×10^{-7} if your calculator can use scientific notation) into the equation for pH for the hydrogen *ion* concentration, $[H^+]$. So, pH = $-\log_{10} [1 \times 10^{-7}]$ will give an answer of 7.0. This is the pH of pure water and is defined as neutral and, as it turns out, it's half way between 0 and 14.

What Affects pH?

A <u>very</u> important pHact to learn is that certain chemicals, when added to water, influence the balance between hydrogen *ions* and hydroxyl *ions*. If the chemical being added reacts with a hydrogen *ion* (such as sodium bicarbonate would), it lowers the overall hydrogen ion concentration. This results in a less acidic solution and a rise in pH (since $[H^+]$ and pH have an inverse relationship). As an example: if $[H^+]$ was to go from 0.00001M (a pH of 5.0) to a smaller value of 0.0000001M (a pH of 7.0).

If the chemical being added to water reacts with a hydroxyl *ion* (such as monobasic sodium phosphate would), it lowers the overall hydroxyl *ion* concentration. This makes the overall hydrogen *ion* concentration higher and results in a more acidic solution and a drop in pH.

Aquarists can (and do) take advantage of this phenomenon to adjust undesired pH values. They can add sodium bicarbonate ($NaHCO_3$ in chemistry shorthand) to raise pH or monobasic sodium phosphate (NaH_2PO_4 in chemistry shorthand) to lower pH. I'll explain this in more detail later in the chapter.

Chapter 2: *pH - The Chemical pHacts*

Since all known life on earth uses water as its solvent, most forms of aquatic life will have a dramatic influence on the chemistry of the surrounding water. As an example, biological filtration slowly acidifies the water as a result of the bacterial conversion of ammonia to nitrate. Conversely, plants and algae use up carbon dioxide during photosynthesis. The carbon dioxide is then removed from the carbonate *equilibria* (discussed in **Chapter 3**) making the water more alkaline. There are many more examples, most of which will be discussed at some point in this chapter or in later chapters.

Signs & Symptoms of pH Problems

Before I go any further, I have to remind you of what I wrote earlier to ensure that you take in its full value. pH is both the most useful and convenient **indicator** of water quality. For the most part, pH is **not** a problem in and of itself. That is, it's an indicator of some other more serious and less obvious underlying problem. A demonstration of this is that often times when you do have what appears to be a pH problem, the results from your attempts at correction will be temporary, if at all. If this is the case, you're probably dealing with some other water quality problem that's manifesting itself as problematic pH. This is a result of the intricate intertwining of pH and the other water qualities.

Keeping this in mind, you can try to use pH to determine what the actual problem is.

Find Related Information at: www.AquaChemPublishing.com

If pH is too low...

buffering capacity: buffering is the resistance of water to a change in pH. Its capacity is based on the number of moles of acid or base required to effect a one unit change in pH.

- ❖ Biological filtration slowly acidifies the aquarium, lowering pH. This will be most evident if the ***buffering capacity*** of the water is very small. If you suspect this, you can either more heavily plant your aquarium (to help complete the Nitrogen Cycle) and/or increase the ***buffering capacity*** of the water by adding sodium bicarbonate.

- ❖ The use of acidic municipal water may result in a low pH aquarium. Again, this will be most evident if the ***buffering capacity*** of the water is small. If you suspect this, test your tap water. If it's acidic, you can either find a different source of water for your aquarium or you can increase the ***buffering capacity*** of your acidic tap water by adding sodium bicarbonate.

Aquarist error may also result in a low pH. If you use the wrong chemical to adjust pH, you may inadvertently lower pH. This will only occur if you have attempted to adjust pH (or some other water quality).

Chapter 2: *pH - The Chemical pHacts*

If pH is too high...

- ❖ Ammonia is a weak base & if its level is high, it will lead to a high pH. This will be most evident if the ***buffering capacity*** of the water is very small. If you suspect this, you should check the ammonia level of your aquarium water. Ammonia is very toxic to fish, so if there is a significant amount of it, you should take steps to remove it immediately (See **Chapter 4**).

  > ***buffering capacity:*** buffering is the resistance of water to a change in pH. Its capacity is based on the number of moles of acid or base required to effect a one unit change in pH.

- ❖ The use of hard water to fill or refill your aquarium can also lead to a high pH. Hard water results from dissolved carbonate salts, such as calcium carbonate ($CaCO_3$ in chemistry shorthand). Some municipal waters are very hard and most well water is extremely hard. If you use well water or suspect your tap water, check its hardness. If you do have hard water, attempting to adjust the pH will usually be futile. Carbonate salts are the main source of ***buffering capacity*** in natural systems. Extremely hard water will be a super buffer. The best way to correct the problem is to perform a partial water change with soft water or to use a water softener in your aquarium (See **Chapter 3**).

Find Related Information at: www.AquaChemPublishing.com

- ❖ An extension of the hard water theme is the ***buffering capacity*** that results from non-carbonate sources. As an example, phosphate salts like monobasic sodium phosphate (mentioned earlier) are also good buffers. The remedy for high pH caused by this type of buffering is a partial water change with soft water. A water softener will **not** affect this problem.

Again, aquarist error may also result in a high pH. If you use the wrong chemical to adjust pH, you may inadvertently raise pH. This will only occur if you have attempted to adjust pH (or some other water quality).

Testing pH

Test kits for pH come in many types and styles. There are pH test strips or pH paper. The paper or strips are dipped in a sample of the aquarium water and the resulting color is compared to a color-gradient pH chart on the packaging. These types are known as "dry" test kits and are quite inexpensive, but usually have moderate accuracy.

There are also "wet" types of pH test kits. To use these kits, you place 4 or 5 milliliters of aquarium water in a small vial and add 2 or 3 drops of a pH indicator. The resulting color of the solution is compared to a color-gradient pH chart on the packaging. This type is slightly more expensive than the previously mentioned types, but it is usually fairly accurate.

Chapter 2: *pH - The Chemical pHacts*

Whichever type of pH test kit you use, either wet or dry, all of them contain some form of pH dependent color indicator. The most common of these indicators is bromothymol blue. This large organic compound has an acid sensitive functional group that interconverts between two forms depending on the pH of the solution. Each form leads to a specific color. When there's a mixture of the forms, the resulting color is a mixture of the two pure colors. Bromothymol blue indicator has a useful pH range from 6.0 (yellow) to 7.6 (blue). So, at pH 6.8 (halfway between the two pH extremes) bromothymol blue indicator will be green.

Other color indicators are also used. But, one thing that all of them have in common is that the colors are sometimes hard to determine with any precision. Unfortunately, your accuracy's all too often dependent on the amount of experience you have with that particular color indicator.

To avoid the confusion that can result from using color indicators, you can test your aquarium pH with a pH meter. To use a pH meter you simply dip it in the aquarium water and read the result on the display. Some meters are slightly more complicated, such as the ones that require calibrating with buffer solutions. While pH meters have a high initial cost (~ 7-10 times that of the wet test kits), they're the most accurate and easy to use method for testing aquarium pH, and can last almost indefinitely if cared for properly.

Correcting pH Mayhem

Adjustments of < 0.5 pH units can be easily accomplished by the simple addition of the proper compound. It's important to note

buffering capacity: buffering is the resistance of water to a change in pH. Its capacity is based on the number of moles of acid or base required to effect a one unit change in pH.

equilibrium: a state in which product formation and reversal to reactants or starting compounds is in balance. An example is that of a bath tub that's being filled while the drain is open. As long as the water pouring in is equal to the water draining out, the water in the bath tub is in a state of equilibrium.

ion: an atom that has gained or lost electrons and, as a result, is charged. i.e. NaCl (table salt) in water exists as Na^{1+} and Cl^{1-}.

though, that it's very difficult (if not impossible) to adjust the pH of a well buffered aquarium. This is because a buffer resists changes in pH. The *buffering capacity* of your aquarium will slowly increase over time, especially if you adjust pH frequently. It's best to periodically perform water changes, even if it doesn't seem that they're needed, to reduce the *buffering capacity*. These water changes will have other beneficial effects that'll be discussed, in turn, in later chapters.

You could adjust pH by adding strong acid or strong base. This should only be done in very small amounts. Strong acids and bases are corrosive and must be handled with great care to prevent personal injury. Unless your aquarium water is well buffered, the addition of either strong acid or strong base must be done very carefully to prevent shock to the aquarium inhabitants from drastic changes in pH. The pH adjusters sold on the market that extol claims like "contains no phosphates" are simply solutions of a strong acid or a strong base. **<u>Important</u>:** Always remember that pH changes must be done in small increments over time. A one unit change in pH is equivalent to a ten-fold change in hydrogen ion concentration, $[H^+]$.

The best way to adjust pH is to add a weak acid or weak base. These compounds are much less corrosive and can be handled safely. In addition, they affect pH in a much more controlled way. They produce *ions* in an *equilibrium*. What this means in practical terms is that they produce partial *ion* concentrations that are less than the total concentration of the non-*ionic* compound (See **Figure 2-3**). This *equilibrium* is pH dependent. As a result, the proportion

Find Related Information at: www.AquaChemPublishing.com

Chapter 2: *pH - The Chemical pHacts*

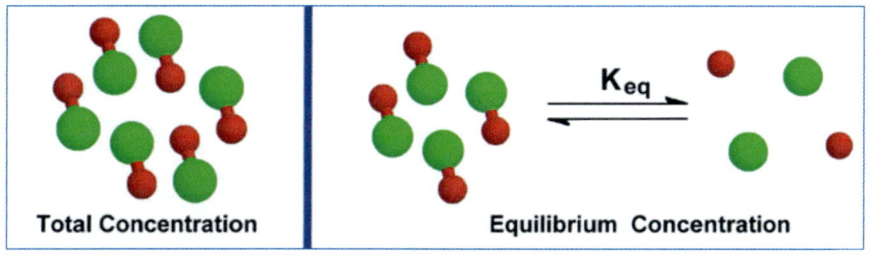

Figure 2-3: An example of an equilibrium. There are a total of six molecules. At equilibrium, 4 of them are still non-ionic & 2 of them have split apart into ions.

of each type of molecule that is present depends on the pH of the solution. If you were to add one of these compounds to pure water of pH 7.0, it would alter the pH based upon its *equilibrium* constant (designated by a "K", such as K_{eq}; in **Figure 2-2** it's a "K_w"). Because these *equilibria* are pH dependent, you can enter their K's as the hydrogen *ion* concentration, [H⁺], in the equation for pH. This results in a new value known as a "pK" which can more easily be related directly to pH. That is, the pK listed for an *equilibrium* is the pH at which the molecules will be in *equilibrium*. As an example: if you enter the K_w from **Figure 2-2** as [H⁺], you get a pK_w of 7.0. This means that at pH 7.0, H^{1+} and OH^{1-} *ions* are in *equilibrium* with their non-*ionic* form of H_2O. In the case of weak acids, the values are written as pK_a's and for weak bases they're written as pK_b's. pK_b's are usually converted to pK_a's (by subtracting the pK_b from 14) to more easily compare them to the pH scale. This is because pK_a can be thought of as the pH at which the hydrogen ion in question will associate (or dissociate, depending on your point of view). On the other hand, a pK_b relates to hydroxyl ions rather than hydrogen ions, so it doesn't relate to pH in a straight forward manner. This may make more sense later.

equilibrium: a state in which product formation and reversal to reactants or starting compounds is in balance. An example is that of a bath tub that's being filled while the drain is open. As long as the water pouring in is equal to the water draining out, the water in the bath tub is in a state of equilibrium.

Find Related Information at: www.AquaChemPublishing.com

To raise pH...

- ❖ you'll need to add a weak base. The most common weak base for aquarium use is sodium bicarbonate ($NaHCO_3$ in chemistry shorthand) and is commonly known as baking soda. Add it in small portions and allow the aquarium water to re-equilibrate for about 15 minutes before testing the pH again. Repeat the process if necessary. (**Note:** If after five or six repetitions there is no change in pH you are probably dealing with well *buffered* water. You'll need to perform a partial water change with soft water and attempt to adjust the pH again, if necessary.)

Sodium bicarbonate has two pK_a's (See **Figure 2-4**). One, for the association of a second hydrogen ion (forming carbonic acid, H_2CO_3), is around pH 6.40. The other, for the dissociation of the hydrogen ion already present (forming a carbonate *ion*, CO_3^{2-}), is around pH 10.25. What this means is that unless the pH is below 6.40 or above 10.25, bicarbonate *ions* (HCO_3^{1-}) will be the predominant species. This also means that the carbonate *equilibria* best maintain a pH between 6.40 and 10.25. It turns out that at ~27°C or 80°F a bicarbonate solution has a pH of around 7.30. This is the perfect pH for biological systems, including fish. (This coincidence is why nature has chosen the carbonate *equilibria* as its main buffering system.)

Chapter 2: *pH - The Chemical pHacts*

$$H_2CO_3 \xrightleftharpoons{pK_a\ 6.40} H^{1+} + HCO_3^{1-}$$

$$HCO_3^{1-} \xrightleftharpoons{pK_a\ 10.25} H^{1+} + CO_3^{2-}$$

Figure 2-4: Equilibria for the carbonate system. A third equilibrium also exists and will be discussed in Chapter 3.

To Lower pH...

- ❖ you'll need to add a weak acid. The most common weak acid for aquarium use is monobasic sodium phosphate (a.k.a. sodium dihydrogen phosphate or, less properly, sodium biphosphate) (NaH_2PO_4 in chemistry shorthand). Add it in small portions and allow the aquarium water to re-equilibrate for about 15 minutes before testing the pH again. Repeat the process if necessary. (**Note:** If after five or six repetitions there is no change in pH you are probably dealing with well **buffered** water. You'll need to perform a partial water change with soft water and attempt to adjust the pH again, if necessary.)

Monobasic sodium phosphate has three pK_a's (See **Figure 2-5**). One, for the association of a third hydrogen ion (forming phosphoric acid, H_3PO_4), is around pH 2.12. Another, for the dissociation of one of the hydrogen **ions** already present (forming a monohydrogen phosphate **ion**, HPO_4^{2-}), is around pH 7.20. The last pK_a is for the dissociation of the other hydrogen **ion** already present

ion: an atom that has gained or lost electrons and, as a result, is charged. i.e. NaCl (table salt) in water exists as Na^{1+} and Cl^{1-}.

Find Related Information at: www.AquaChemPublishing.com

$$H_3PO_4 \underset{\longleftarrow}{\overset{pK_a\ 2.12}{\longrightarrow}} H^{1+} + H_2PO_4^{1-}$$

$$H_2PO_4^{1-} \underset{\longleftarrow}{\overset{pK_a\ 7.20}{\longrightarrow}} H^{1+} + HPO_4^{2-}$$

$$HPO_4^{2-} \underset{\longleftarrow}{\overset{pK_a\ 12.66}{\longrightarrow}} H^{1+} + PO_4^{3-}$$

Figure 2-5: Equilibria for the phosphate system. Because phosphate has three pH dependent equilibria, it is an extremely good buffering system.

forming a phosphate ion, PO_4^{3-}) and is around pH 12.66. What this means is that if the pH is below 7.20 dihydrogen phosphate *ions* ($H_2PO_4^{1-}$) will predominate, and if it's above 7.20, monohydrogen phosphate *ions* (HPO_4^{2-}) will predominate. This also means that the phosphate *equilibria* can maintain a wide range of pH. At ~27°C or 80°F a 5% dihydrogen phosphate solution has a pH of around 4.18. **Note:** A possible side effect from using phosphates to adjust pH is that high concentrations of phosphates lead to increased algal growth on the aquarium glass and, in extreme cases, to algal blooms. This is only the case with blue-green algae. Excess brown algal growth results from other excesses, such as overfeeding. Some aquarists feel that algae on the aquarium glass is visually unappealing and interferes with the viewing of their fish. While this may be true, the algae isn't harmful to the fish and can actually serve as a source of food for certain species. It's important to note, though, that the algae can use up important nutrients and carbon dioxide that higher plants in your aquarium need. If your aquarium

Chapter 2: *pH - The Chemical pHacts*

is planted with immortal plastic plants, there's obviously no need for concern.

The aquarium industry has responded to these concerns and now markets non-phosphate pH adjusters. As mentioned earlier, these products claim, and correctly so, that they "contain no phosphates". They aren't anything new or extraordinary, though. They're just solutions of strong acid (usually sulfuric acid, H_2SO_4) or strong base (usually sodium hydroxide, NaOH). These solutions are very corrosive and must be handled with great care to prevent personal injury. Unless your aquarium water is well ***buffered***, their addition must be done very carefully to prevent shock to the aquarium inhabitants from drastic changes in pH. You'd be much better advised to ascertain why you need to adjust your pH to begin with and correct that problem instead.

For instance, if your pH is consistently 7.6 and you add monobasic sodium phosphate every week to lower the pH to 7.1, you'll end up with an aquarium with fairly high phosphate concentrations. Undoubtedly, you'll eventually have blue-green algae growing all over your aquarium. As an added insult to your injury, you'll be spending plenty of your hobby money on pH adjuster. Instead of this unpleasant scenario, you could test your aquarium water for ammonia and hardness. It turns out that your pH is 7.6 because you've been using hard tap water to fill and refill your aquarium. You invest in a water softener for your aquarium (only the cost of two months of phosphate pH adjuster). As a result, you very rarely need to adjust your pH and your blue-green algae problem is eliminated.

Find Related Information at: www.AquaChemPublishing.com

If, for some reason, you still have a need to add corrosive chemicals to your aquarium, be careful. **Important:** pH changes must be done in small increments over time. A one unit change in pH is equivalent to a ten-fold change in hydrogen ion concentration, $[H^+]$.

One Final pHact

As mentioned earlier, the *buffering capacity* of your aquarium will slowly increase over time, especially if you adjust pH frequently. If you're always adding sodium bicarbonate and monobasic sodium phosphate without ever removing any of them, they will become more and more concentrated. Compounds that have multiple *equilibria*, like the ones you add to adjust pH, produce a buffering effect, and as they become more concentrated, the water's capacity to buffer will increase. Remember to periodically perform water changes to reduce the *buffering capacity* so that any pH problems you do experience will be much easier to correct.

Siamese Fighting Fish (*Betta splendens*) can be kept in a community aquarium as long as there is only one male.

Find Related Information at: www.AquaChemPublishing.com

Chapter 2: *pH - The Chemical pHacts*

Chapter At-A-Glance

- pH is the measure of acidity or alkalinity of a solution on a scale from 0 (most acidic) to 14 (most alkaline).
- Range for aquaria: ~6.0-8.0.
- Expressed as: $pH = -\log_{10}[H^+]$

- Just about everything in an aquarium affects and is affected by pH.

- Symptoms of pH problems.
    - If pH is too low...
        - from long term biological filtration and/or short term biological filtration with low buffering capacity.
        - from acidic municipal tap water.
    - Remedy:
        - Add sodium bicarbonate or perform a partial water change with hard water.
    - If pH is too high...
        - from ammonia from incomplete biological filtration.
        - from the use of extremely hard water to fill or refill aquarium.
        - from non-carbonate buffering sources.
    - Remedy:
        - Remove ammonia, soften water, and/or add monobasic sodium phosphate. In extreme cases, perform partial water changes with soft water.

- pH testing:
    - "wet" kit: done with 4 or 5 milliliters of aquarium water and pH dependent color indicator.
    - "dry" kit: done with sample of aquarium water and dipping strip.
- pH meter: dip in aquarium water.

Find Related Information at: www.AquaChemPublishing.com

- Adjusting pH:
    - Must always be done in small increments over time. A One unit change in pH is equal to a ten-fold change in [H^+] concentration.
    - Add sodium bicarbonate or sodium hydroxide to raise pH.
    - Add monobasic sodium phosphate or sulfuric acid to lower pH.

- Buffering capacity arises from high concentrations of compounds that exist in multiple equilibria. It results in difficult, if not impossible, pH adjustments.
    - Perform periodic partial water changes to lower buffering capacity.

Chapter 3: *Water Hardness*

Water Hardness

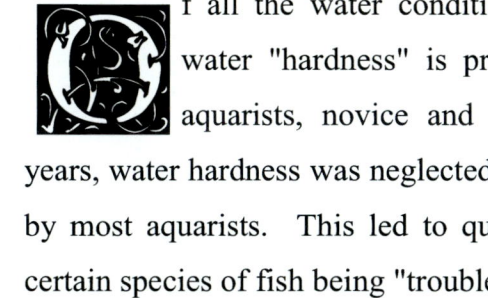f all the water conditions that occur in an aquarium, water "hardness" is probably the least understood by aquarists, novice and experienced, alike. For many years, water hardness was neglected, sometimes completely ignored, by most aquarists. This led to quite a few misconceptions about certain species of fish being "trouble" fish or being difficult to breed. Even though our understanding of water hardness has grown over the years, most aquarists still don't know what it is, much less what to do about it.

Lessening The Confusion

Most of the confusion about water hardness arises from the sheer magnitude of terms used to describe it, many of which are synonyms. Usually, the initial confusion arises from the fact that hardness can be measured either in ***parts per million*** (ppm) or in DH units. Each DH unit is equivalent to 17.8 ***ppm***. DH, or Deutsche Hartgrad, loosely translated, means German hardness gradient, however most aquarists think of DH as "<u>D</u>egrees of <u>H</u>ardness" or <u>G</u>erman <u>D</u>egrees of <u>H</u>ardness (GDH). As a result of the different systems, it's not uncommon to see water hardness **<u>incorrectly</u>**

parts per million (ppm): one part of compound in question in one million parts of solvent. This is equivalent to milligrams per liter ($^{mg}/_L$).

Find Related Information at: www.AquaChemPublishing.com

reported as DH = 85 ppm (an erroneous combination of both systems).

If you wade your way through this initial onslaught of confusion, there's plenty of waves of it to follow in the sub-categories of water hardness. Most of these terms are listed in **Figure 3-2**. Any synonymous terms are listed directly below their counterparts.

What Makes Water Hard?

Well then, what is this condition we call "hardness" and how do we know if our aquarium water "has" it? As mentioned in **Chapter 1**, water hardness in natural waters comes from rainwater filtering down through geological formations, such as limestone, on its journey to the earth's water table. During this trip the water absorbs inorganic salts from these geological formations. The main *cations* acquired on the trip are: calcium (Ca^{2+}), magnesium (Mg^{2+}), iron (Fe^{3+}), and some aluminum (Al^{3+}). The main *anions* acquired are: carbonate (CO_3^{2-}), sulfate (SO_4^{2-}), chloride (Cl^{1-}), and some nitrate (NO_3^{1-}). Depending on the geology of the region where you live, your water can have a water hardness rating anywhere from soft (few dissolved salts) to extremely hard (many dissolved salts).

cation: (kat-ion) a positively charged ion.
anion: (ann-ion) a negatively charged ion.

Actual "hardness" comes from the multivalent (more than one unit of charge) *cation* portions of the inorganic salts, mostly calcium (Ca^{2+}) and magnesium (Mg^{2+}), when in solution. The majority of these salts (~ 80% or more) are carbonate salts, like calcium carbonate ($CaCO_3$, limestone) and magnesium carbonate ($MgCO_3$). Sulfate and chloride salts, like magnesium sulfate

Find Related Information at: www.AquaChemPublishing.com

Chapter 3: *Water Hardness*

($MgSO_4$, gypsum) and calcium chloride ($CaCl_2$), usually account for the remainder.

Because hardness mainly arises from carbonate salts, it's usually reported in ***ppm*** $CaCO_3$. And, because these salts are also principally responsible for the chemistry related to water hardness, they need to be elaborated in greater detail, later in the chapter. (See **Figure 3-1** for some hardness ranges.)

parts per million (ppm): one part of compound in question in one million parts of solvent. This is equivalent to milligrams per liter ($^{mg}/_L$).

Hardness	ppm	DH
Very Soft	0-30	0-1.5
Soft	30-100	1.5-5.5
Hard	100-250	5.5-14.0
Very Hard	above 250	above 14.0

Figure 3-1: Some typical ranges for aquarium water General Hardness (GH), shown in both ppm and DH units.

An obvious source for water hardness in your aquarium is that the water was already hard when you filled the aquarium. What if your tap water isn't hard, but somehow your aquarium water is? It's important to keep less obvious sources of water hardness in mind. The most prominent of these is untreated ornamental rock. Rocks are mineral deposits, and these minerals can leach into your aquarium water if left untreated. Not ALL minerals will leach, and so not all rocks must be treated. But before you go putting some rocks you found lying around in your aquarium, do your homework. Try to determine what kind of rock it is. It's very likely that you'll be able to determine this with a little help from your local library. If you're still not sure, you can put the rock in some vinegar water for a week or so to see if the hardness levels rise. If not, the rock is probably safe to put in your aquarium.

Find Related Information at: www.AquaChemPublishing.com

The Water Hardness Vocabulary

To attempt to alleviate much of the confusion about water hardness, it's necessary to survey the many terms used to describe it as a whole, or in part. Once you're familiar with the vocabulary of water hardness, its chemistry will be much easier to understand.

Beginning with the whole:

The overall sum of multivalent *cations* is known as "General Hardness" (GH) or "Total Hardness". This is what water hardness test kits measure, unless otherwise indicated. In the early days of water testing, this used to be determined with a bottle, laundry detergent, and a "fudge factor". The hardness was based on how sudsy the water became when it was shaken with laundry detergent in a bottle. Obviously, this was a very subjective technique. Today there are extremely accurate chemical methods for determining hardness to within 1 or 2 ppm.

The whole is the sum of the parts:

General Hardness is comprised of two parts: 1) "Carbonate Hardness" (KH), and 2) "Non-Carbonate Hardness" (non-KH or NKH). (The K in KH comes from the German spelling of carbonate.)

So…

$$\mathbf{GH = KH + non\text{-}KH}$$

Find Related Information at: www.AquaChemPublishing.com

Chapter 3: *Water Hardness*

Carbonate Hardness (KH):

Carbonate hardness has an intimate relationship with pH and is known synonymously as, ***buffering capacity***. It is also **erroneously** known as "alkalinity" because of its ability to maintain an alkaline pH. Yet another term for KH arises from the fact that it is influenced by carbon dioxide exchange. An early method for 'removing' carbonate hardness was to boil off the carbon dioxide, rendering the carbonate salts insoluble. Because of this changeable state of carbonate hardness, KH is also known as "Temporary Hardness".

buffering capacity: buffering is the resistance of water to a change in pH. Its capacity is based on the number of moles of acid or base required to effect a one unit change in pH.

Non-Carbonate Hardness (non-KH):

The other salts of calcium and magnesium, like calcium chloride ($CaCl_2$) or magnesium sulfate ($MgSO_4$), are freely soluble in water and aren't affected by boiling. Because of this persisting state, non-KH is also known as "Permanent Hardness". The majority of this type of hardness stems from sulfate salts, so yet another term used to describe it is "Sulfate Hardness".

As you can see, the big picture of water hardness has many facets. It's easy to see why so much confusion exists. From this point on, only the terms in the first line of **Figure 3-2** will be used. Hopefully, this attempt to standardize the terms used will help to lessen the confusion surrounding water hardness and clarify its chemistry.

Find Related Information at: www.AquaChemPublishing.com

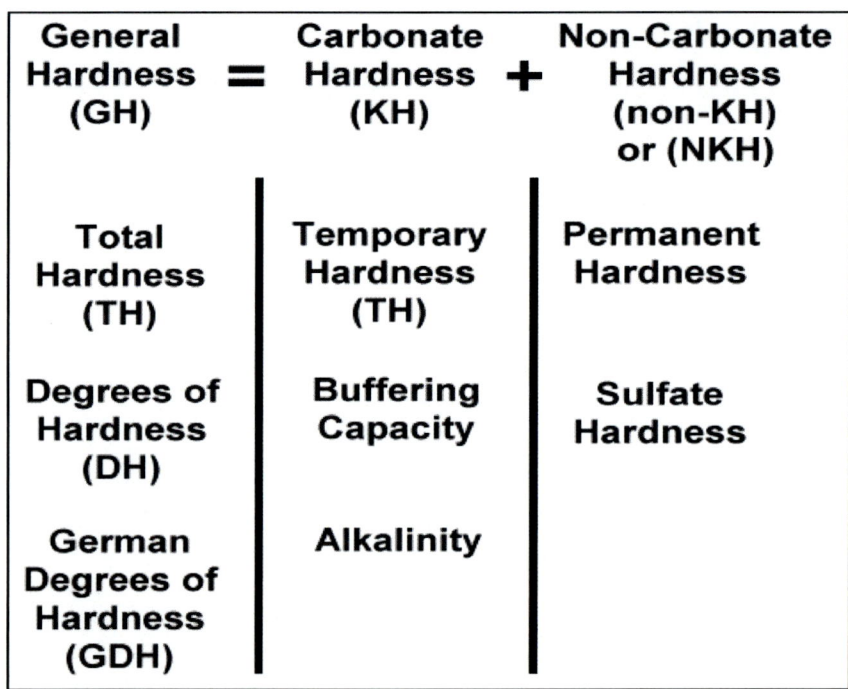

Figure 3-2: The big picture of Water Hardness, including all of the synonyms for each term listed below their respective counterparts.

Signs & Symptoms of Hardness Problems

An extremely common sign of water hardness is a crusty off-white film that develops on the aquarium glass, just above the water line. This scaling is a direct result of the carbonate salts that are the main component of hardness. The film develops because calcium and magnesium carbonate ($CaCO_3$ & $MgCO_3$) are nearly insoluble in water. When they're in solution, they exist mainly as bicarbonate salts ($Ca(HCO_3)_2$ & $Mg(HCO_3)_2$), which are freely soluble in water (See **Figure 3-3**). As the water evaporates, the *equilibrium* in **Figure 3-3** shifts toward the carbonate side and the insoluble carbonate salts precipitate. This also occurs if the water is boiled and the carbon dioxide (CO_2) is driven off. Tea drinkers will

equilibrium: a state in which product formation and reversal to reactants or starting compounds is in balance. An example is that of a bath tub that's being filled while the drain is open. As long as the water pouring in is equal to the water draining out, the water in the bath tub is in a state of equilibrium.

Chapter 3: *Water Hardness*

probably recognize this from the scaling that deposits in their teapots.

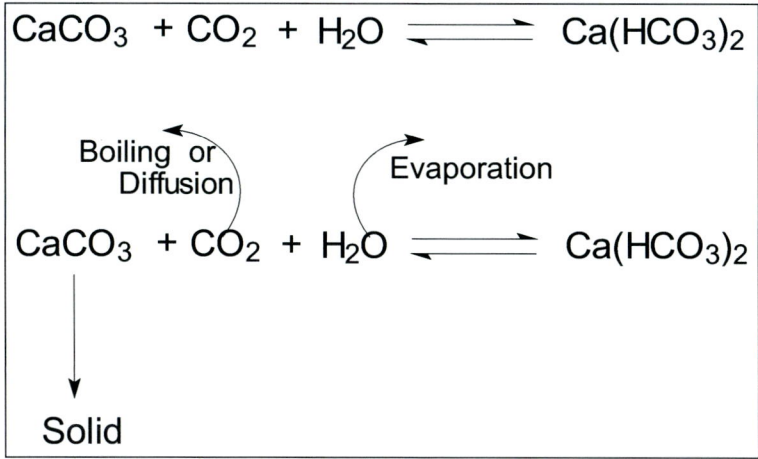

Figure 3-3: Solubility equilibrium for calcium carbonate showing that if either water (H_2O) is removed by evaporation or carbon dioxide (CO_2) is removed by boiling, the resulting insoluble calcium carbonate that is produced will precipitate (form solid).

The scaling that results from hardness is only a small part of its chemistry. The carbonate salts also exist in a second set of *equilibria*, known fittingly as the carbonate *equilibria*. (See **Figure 3-4**) The upper portion of the figure shows that a molecule of carbon dioxide (CO_2) is required for calcium carbonate ($CaCO_3$) to dissolve. Once dissolved, the calcium bicarbonate ($Ca(HCO_3)_2$) completely dissociates (breaks apart) into its respective *ions*, a calcium *ion* (Ca^{2+}) and two bicarbonate *ions* (HCO_3^{1-}). Once the bicarbonate ions have formed, they can participate in the pH dependent *equilibria* in the lower portion of the figure. What's meant by pH dependence, in practical terms, is that the *equilibria* affect pH and are affected by pH. Because of this, hardness from carbonate salts imparts a property known as **buffering capacity**.

equilibrium: a state in which product formation and reversal to reactants or starting compounds is in balance. An example is that of a bath tub that's being filled while the drain is open. As long as the water pouring in is equal to the water draining out, the water in the bath tub is in a state of equilibrium.

ion: an atom that has gained or lost electrons and, as a result, is charged. i.e. NaCl (table salt) in water exists as Na^{1+} and Cl^{1-}.

Find Related Information at: www.AquaChemPublishing.com

The water will resist a change in pH because there are several steps that involve hydrogen *ion* (H^{1+}) association or dissociation.

$$CaCO_3 + CO_2 + H_2O \rightleftharpoons Ca(HCO_3)_2$$

$$Ca(HCO_3)_2 \longrightarrow Ca^{2+} + 2\,HCO_3^{1-}$$

Dissolving / Diffusing

$$CO_2 + H_2O \longrightarrow H_2CO_3$$

$$H_2CO_3 \underset{}{\overset{pK_a\ 6.40}{\rightleftharpoons}} H^{1+} + HCO_3^{1-}$$

$$HCO_3^{1-} \underset{}{\overset{pK_a\ 10.25}{\rightleftharpoons}} H^{1+} + CO_3^{2-}$$

Figure 3-4: The carbonate equilibria showing the importance of carbon dioxide (CO_2) and their dependence upon pH.

pKa: the negative base ten log of a weak acid's dissociation constant. This is done to allow quick, easy comparison to the pH scale. In practical terms, pKa can be thought of as the pH at which the hydrogen ion (H^{1+}) in question will associate or dissociate.

Because of the *pKₐ*'s of carbonic acid (H_2CO_3) and bicarbonate (HCO_3^{1-}), shown in **Figure 3-4**, water with appreciable amounts of carbonate salts maintains an alkaline pH, around 7.4. As a result of its uncanny ability to maintain alkalinity, the term has become **erroneously** synonymous with carbonate hardness.

So, if you have scaling deposits on the aquarium glass, or an alkaline pH despite attempts at its correction, you should consider water hardness the likely source of the problems.

Another important aspect of KH is it's relation to carbon dioxide (CO_2), shown in **Figure 3-4**. Aquatic plants utilize carbon dioxide during photosynthesis to produce sugars which the plant will

Chapter 3: *Water Hardness*

later use for energy. In order for these plants to survive and grow, there must be a minimum amount (5-6 ppm) of carbon dioxide dissolved in the aquarium water. There are a few species of aquatic plants that can also utilize atmospheric carbon dioxide, however in order to do so they mustn't be fully submerged. This isn't really practical in an aquarium, so dissolved carbon dioxide is essentially the only source used by aquarium-based aquatic plants.

The solubility of carbon dioxide in water is based upon a number of key factors such as surface area, temperature, pH, and KH. With respect to an aquarium, the temperature range is narrow enough to make it of little consequence. Most aquaria are outfitted with air stones or filters that sufficiently agitate the water's surface making this factor also of little consequence. From a practical perspective, pH and KH are the predominating factors controlling how much dissolved carbon dioxide is available to planted aquaria. The amount of dissolved carbon dioxide can be determined from a solubility table (see **Figure 3-5**).

KH (ppm)	17.8	35.6	53.4	71.2	89	107	125	142	160	178	196	214
pH \ DH	1	2	3	4	5	6	7	8	9	10	11	12
6.50	11	21	31	40	50	59	68	77	86	94	103	111
6.75	6	12	17	23	28	33	38	43	48	53	58	63
7.00	3	7	10	13	16	19	21	24	27	30	33	35
7.25	2	4	5	7	9	10	12	14	15	17	18	20
7.50	1	2	3	4	5	6	7	8	9	9	10	11
7.75	1	1	2	2	3	3	4	4	5	5	6	6
8.00	0.3	0.7	1	1.3	1.6	1.8	2.1	2.4	2.7	3	3.2	3.5

Figure 3-5: A Table for determining the concentration (in ppm) of dissolved carbon dioxide at 25°C (77°F) based on the aquarium pH and KH.

Find Related Information at: www.AquaChemPublishing.com

If your aquarium has a pH of 7.25 and a KH of 89 ppm, you can see from the table in **Figure 3-5** that there is 9 ppm of dissolved carbon dioxide available in the water for aquatic plants. In order to maintain a healthy level of dissolved carbon dioxide (5-15 ppm) for aquatic plants, you will need to target a pH of 7.0-7.5 and a KH of 70-160 ppm.

Testing Water Hardness

Test kits for carbonate hardness (KH) and general hardness (GH) come in many types and styles. There are hardness test strips. The strips are dipped in a sample of the aquarium water and the resulting color is compared to a color-gradient chart on the packaging. These types are known as "dry" test kits and are quite inexpensive, but usually have moderate accuracy.

There are also "wet" types of hardness test kits. For KH, one usually places 4 or 5 milliliters of aquarium water in a small vial and adds an acid (often mixed with a pH dependent indicator) dropwise until a desired color change occurs. Based on the number of drops added and the concentration of the acid, the KH can be calculated. For GH, one usually places 4 or 5 milliliters of aquarium water in a test vial and adds 2 or 3 drops of base to ensure an alkaline pH. Following this, 2 or 3 drops of a magnesium-dependent indicator is added. A chemical that "ties up" the *ions* that cause hardness (usually EDTA) is then added dropwise until the indicator changes color. Based on the number of drops added and the concentration of the EDTA solution, the GH can be calculated. "Wet" type test kits are slightly more expensive than the previously mentioned "dry" type, but they are usually fairly accurate.

Chapter 3: *Water Hardness*

The most common of the "wet" types of kits that measures general hardness (GH) is one that employs an EDTA (ethylenediamine tetraacetic acid) *titration* using calmagite as an indicator. The test is performed by taking a sample of aquarium water and adding strong base, to ~ pH 10. Several drops of calmagite indicator, a large organic molecule, are added. This forms a wine red solution. A solution of EDTA of known concentration is added dropwise until the test solution's color changes from wine red to blue -- the endpoint. Based on the EDTA concentration and the volume of it added, the hardness (in ***ppm***) can be determined. This value can then be converted to DH units if so desired.

Calmagite is used as the indicator because it conveniently forms a wine red colored complex with magnesium ***ions***, but forms no colored complex with calcium ***ions***. It also happens that EDTA forms a much stronger complex with calcium than with magnesium. So, EDTA complexes calcium ***ion***s <u>before</u> magnesium ***ions***. Once all of the calcium ***ions*** are complexed, the magnesium ***ions*** begin to complex. As this progresses, the wine red color from the magnesium-calmagite complex disappears and the endpoint (blue) is reached.

Softening Hard Water

So, how do you get rid of your hard water problems? For general hardness (GH), there are essentially two ways to "soften" your water. The first is to effect a partial water change using distilled or de-ionized water. If you remove some of the water that is hard and replace it with soft water, the overall hardness of the aquarium water will be lessened.

titration: the use of a known chemical reaction to determine the concentration of one of the reactants. Some sort of visual indicator is usually used to display the endpoint of the reaction. For example, an unknown amount of acid can be determined with a known amount of base and a pH indicator. Once all of the acid is reacted with base, the indicator changes color.

ion: an atom that has gained or lost electrons and, as a result, is charged. i.e. NaCl (table salt) in water exists as Na^{1+} and Cl^{1-}.

Find Related Information at: www.AquaChemPublishing.com

The second is to add either naturally occurring zeolite rock or synthetic ion-exchange resin to your filter medium. Both zeolite rock and ion-exchange resin act by exchanging sodium *ions* (Na^{1+}) for those intolerable multivalent metal *ions* (mostly Ca^{2+} and Mg^{2+}) and both zeolite and ion-exchange resin can be regenerated by soaking them in a concentrated sodium chloride (table salt) solution for a day or so. In extreme hard water cases, you can use both methods simultaneously to more quickly lower an exceptionally high GH.

For carbonate hardness (KH), there are also two ways to "soften" your water. The first is to add a strong acid (hydrochloric or sulfuric acid) until the **buffering capacity** is depleted. This doesn't actually remove the carbonate hardness, it just negates it so that it doesn't influence pH any longer.

buffering capacity: buffering is the resistance of water to a change in pH. Its capacity is based on the number of moles of acid or base required to effect a one unit change in pH.

The second method is to perform a partial water change with distilled or de-ionized water. Replacing the carbonate laden aquarium water with "soft", carbonate-free water will lessen the overall carbonate concentration in your aquarium. Unlike the previous method, this technique does remove the actual source of the hardness, and as a result, is often preferred.

A few words of caution regarding water hardness adjustments: water changes can be done with distilled water as long as it's no more than ~10-20% at one time. Any more than this may cause undue stress for the aquarium inhabitants, especially for sensitive species. Complete removal of all hardness should probably be avoided. That is, a large portion of the **buffering capacity** of your aquarium water will be destroyed by the "softening" process. This can lead to pH problems. If the **buffering**

Find Related Information at: www.AquaChemPublishing.com

Chapter 3: *Water Hardness*

capacity has reached its maximum or minimum limit, drastic changes in pH can occur. The buffer can only absorb so much acid or base while maintaining the same pH. Once the maximum or minimum capacity is reached, pH will change drastically. These drastic pH changes cause great stress in the fish which can lessen their ability to resist disease. If the changes are LARGE enough (3 or 4 pH units), the fish can experience pH shock, leading to their death.

So, monitor the softening process daily. Once the hardness levels reach an acceptable value, stop the process. That is, either don't perform any more water changes with distilled water, or remove the ion-exchanging materials from the aquarium.

Lyretail Black Mollies (*Xiphophorus maculates*) are nice livebearers for a community aquarium.

Find Related Information at: www.AquaChemPublishing.com

Chapter At-A-Glance

- General Hardness (GH) is the measure of multivalent metal ions, mostly calcium (Ca^{2+}) and magnesium (Mg^{2+}).
    - Most of these ions are from carbonate salts.
    - Because carbonate salts have their own chemistry, they are an important part of general hardness known as carbonate hardness, or KH.
    - The portion of general hardness not arising from carbonate salts is known as non-carbonate hardness, or non-KH.
    - GH = KH + non-KH

- Symptoms of Water Hardness:
    - A high amount of carbonate hardness will present itself as a crusty off-white film on the aquarium glass, just above the waterline.

- Softening Hard Water:
    - There are three ways to soften hard water (KH and GH):
        1) Perform partial water changes with "soft" water (distilled water). Effective for <u>BOTH</u> KH & GH.
        2) Remove the offending multivalent ions by adding either zeolite rock or synthetic ion-exchange resin to your filter medium. Effective for GH <u>ONLY</u>.
        3) Add strong acid (hydrochloric or sulfuric acid) to deplete the buffering capacity. Effective for KH <u>ONLY</u>.

- Testing Water Hardness:
    - "dry" kit: done with sample of aquarium water and a dipping strip.
    - "wet" kit: done with 4 or 5 milliliters of aquarium water and either acid titration with pH dependent color indicator (KH), or EDTA titration with magnesium dependent color indicator (GH).

Find Related Information at: www.AquaChemPublishing.com

Chapter 4: *The Nitrogen Cycle*

The Nitrogen Cycle

here's a great deal of chemistry occurring in an aquarium, but none may be more important than the nitrogen cycle. This chemistry is constantly in motion, in a healthy aquarium, anyway. And, if the cycle is interrupted at any point, there could be dire consequences. It's almost impossible to maintain an aquarium and its inhabitants without a properly cycling nitrogen cycle.

The Making of A Cycle

The nitrogen cycle is nature's way of getting nitrogen (N_2 in chemistry shorthand) from one organism to another -- nitrogen recycling of sorts. Each organism takes in (eats, absorbs, etc.) nitrogen in one form and puts out (excretes, desorbs, etc.) nitrogen in another form. For example, fish take in nitrogen in the form of protein (containing amino acids) and excrete nitrogen in the form of ammonia in there urine. This ammonia is now available to other organisms as their nitrogen source. If enough organisms participate in this process, a complete cycle can be formed in which the nitrogen is continually recycling. This is what occurs in a balanced aquatic environment.

Find Related Information at: www.AquaChemPublishing.com

We will begin explaining the nitrogen cycle (see **Figure 4-1**) in detail with the role that fish play (since it's a cycle, you could begin the explanation at any point). The fish take in nitrogen in the form of protein from any of a number of sources: plants, tubifex worms, brine shrimp, flaked foods, etc. After the protein has been broken down and the fish absorbs the needed nutrients, the excess nitrogen is excreted in its urine and feces. The urine contains

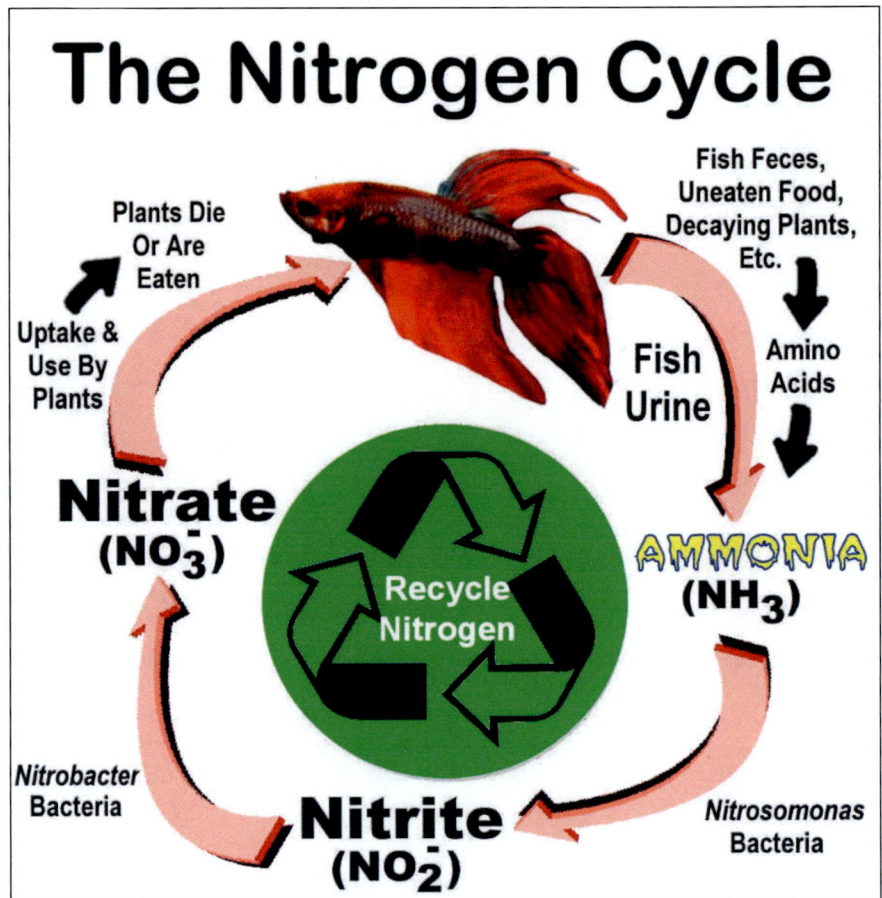

Figure 4-1: The Nitrogen Cycle in an aquarium. At least 2 different organisms are needed for proper function.

ammonia and the feces contain amino acids and partially digested protein. Decaying plants, decaying fish, uneaten food, fish feces,

Chapter 4: *The Nitrogen Cycle*

etc. are converted to ammonia by bacteria. The ammonia (NH_3 in chemistry shorthand) can then be oxidized (converted) to nitrite (NO_2^{1-} in chemistry shorthand) by *Nitrosomonas* bacteria. The nitrite is further oxidized to nitrate (NO_3^{1-} in chemistry shorthand) by *Nitrobacter* bacteria. The nitrate can then be absorbed by terrestrial based plants that live in or near the water. It's interesting to note that most aquatic plants absorb ammonia directly (as ammonium ion, NH_4^{1+} in chemistry shorthand), greatly shortening the nitrogen cycle.

The portion of the nitrogen cycle that deals with the conversion of ammonia to nitrates is also known as biological filtration. Biological filters exist wherever bacteria (*Nitrosomonas* and *Nitrobacter*) can colonize. This usually occurs in the gravel of an aquarium, on activated carbon in a filter, or on Bio-Wheels that are specifically added to a filter for bacterial colonization.

Diagram of A Cycle

Ammonia (NH_3):

One of the most immediate dangers to the fish in your aquarium is that of ammonia poisoning. Simply put, ammonia kills by suffocation -- it literally drowns your fish. This happens as a result of the ability of ammonia to irreversibly bind to fish hemoglobin in a fish's oxygen-carrying red blood cells. Once this binding occurs, blood cells are no longer able to transport oxygen throughout the fish's body. This, in turn, leads to a systemic failure in the victim, and ultimately death. It's very similar to cyanide poisoning in humans. Suffocation occurs even though there is an ample supply of oxygen present -- a tragic and preventable death.

Find Related Information at: www.AquaChemPublishing.com

The only way to prevent such a tragedy is to keep a constant vigil as to the ammonia levels in your aquarium. This is of absolute importance in a newly setup aquarium. The biological filter hasn't had time to become established, so ammonia levels elevate quickly. Eventually the ammonia levels fall to normal as nitrite levels spike. This is followed by nitrite levels falling to zero as nitrate levels gradually increase. This is commonly known as "The Break-In Cycle", "New Tank Syndrome", or "The Conditioning Period" (see **Figure 4-2**).

Even in an established aquarium, ammonia levels can spike (say from the external biological filter becoming clogged, or from the death and decomposition of a large plant or fish). So regularly monitoring ammonia levels is a must, and immediate remedy of any spikes is equally as important.

Nitrite (NO_2^{1-}):

During the initial cycling of your aquarium (see **Figure 4-2**), nitrite levels will rise rapidly as the ammonia is converted by the growing *Nitrosomonas* population. Nitrite is much less toxic to fish than ammonia, however it can still damage gill tissue and produce undue stress. As long as the nitrogen cycle is functioning properly, the nitrite will be converted fairly quickly to nitrate and so it poses only a small threat to your fish.

Nitrate (NO_3^{1-}):

In the later stages of the nitrogen cycle, nitrate is formed by *Nitrobacter* bacteria from nitrite. Nitrate levels will gradually increase over time (see **Figure 4-2**). Terrestrial based plants that can live in an aquarium or a select few species of aquatic plants (i.e.

Hornwort) can absorb the nitrate for conversion into plant proteins. These plants then either die or are eaten by fish, and the nitrogen cycle begins again.

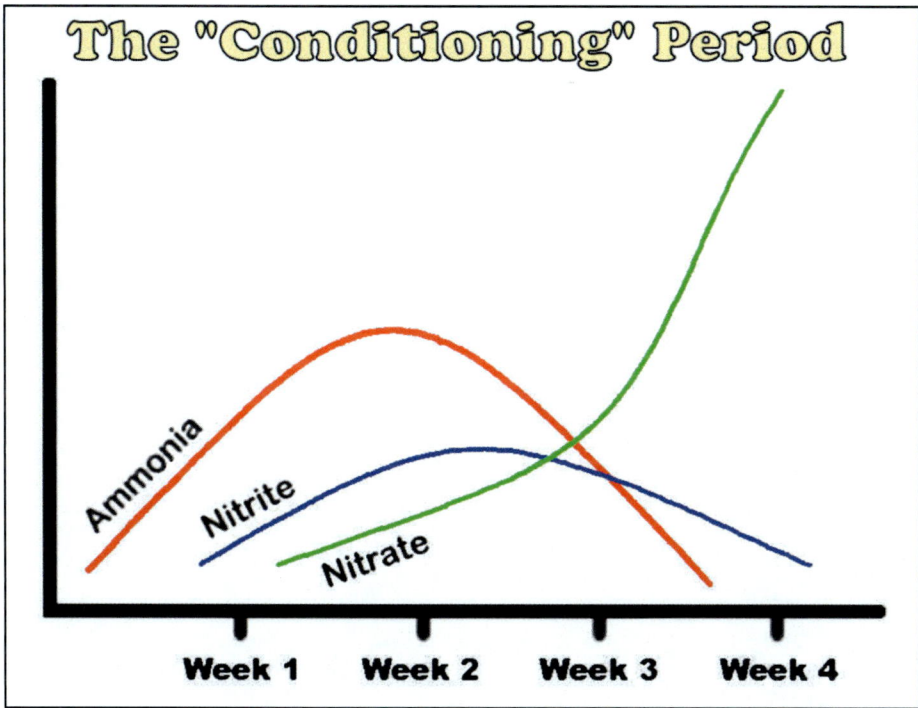

Figure 4-2: A diagram of the "conditioning" period of an aquarium. This is also known as "The Break-In Cycle" or "New Tank Syndrome". <u>NOTE</u>: The timeline shown in the diagram is **approximate** and is dependent on both temperature and concentration.

Products are available that are purported by their manufacturers to greatly shorten the conditioning period, all but eliminating the occurrence of New Tank Syndrome. Just a few of them are: Biozyme® made by Aquarium Products, Nutrafin Cycle® made by Hagen, and Drs. Foster & Smith Water Repair System – Colonize®. All of these products contain live nitrifying bacteria in one form or another to jump start the nitrogen cycle in a new aquarium.

Signs & Symptoms of A Broken Cycle

A broken nitrogen cycle is rather difficult to diagnose. There are many symptoms that can be attributed to it as well as many other aquarium chemistry disorders. For instance, the nitrogen cycle is continually acidifying the aquarium water, but unless the aquarist is aware of this fact, one might think that their aquarium has a pH problem. As another example, some species of fish (i.e. barbs) are sensitive to high levels of nitrates. They may appear lethargic and unhealthy. Unless the aquarist is aware of the nitrate levels in their aquarium, they may think that a disease outbreak has occurred and begin treating the aquarium haphazardly for various diseases.

The problem with diagnosing a broken nitrogen cycle is that there are no real visible signs of the problem. There are only indirect indicators of the underlying problem, like those described above. As a result, the aquarist must rely on test kits to monitor the levels of ammonia, nitrites, and nitrates in their aquarium.

Testing Ammonia

parts per million (ppm): one part of compound in question in one million parts of solvent. This is equivalent to milligrams per liter ($^{mg}/_L$).

The simplest and most common ammonia test kit is one that uses Nessler's Reagent, or a slightly modified version of it. With this type of kit, you place a known volume of aquarium water (usually 4-6 milliliters) in a clear test vial. Three to eight drops of Nessler's Reagent is then added to the test vial. After 2-3 minutes, the resulting color of the solution is compared to a color gradient total ammonia chart to determine the concentration in either ***ppm***-NH_3 or ***ppm***-N(itrogen). Variants of these types of kits also exist in which the liquid indicator is replaced by a powdered, granular, or tablet form of indicator.

Find Related Information at: www.AquaChemPublishing.com

Chapter 4: *The Nitrogen Cycle*

Nessler's Reagent is an alkaline mercuric iodide solution (OH^{1-} / HgI_2). The alkalai (OH^{1-}) is present to convert any ammonium ion (NH_4^{1+}) to free ammonia (NH_3). As a result, this test type measures total ammonia ONLY. To determine free ammonia with this test type, a conversion chart that is based upon pH and temperature must be used (see **Figure 4-3**). This can be fairly significant since free ammonia is toxic to fish but ammonium ion is nontoxic. As an example, you may determine a total ammonia level of 2 *ppm* (*parts per million*) at a pH of 7.5 and a temperature of 79°F (~26°C). Using **Figure 4-3**, the pH and temperature intersect at 1.89. What this means is that 1.89% of the total ammonia is in

Temp (°C)	20	21	22	23	24	25	26	27	28	29	30
pH °F	68	69.8	71.6	73.4	75.2	77	78.8	80.6	82.4	84.2	86
6.0	0.040	0.043	0.046	0.049	0.053	0.057	0.061	0.065	0.070	0.075	0.080
6.5	0.125	0.135	0.145	0.156	0.167	0.180	0.193	0.207	0.221	0.237	0.254
7.0	0.396	0.425	0.457	0.491	0.527	0.566	0.607	0.651	0.697	0.747	0.799
7.5	1.24	1.33	1.43	1.54	1.65	1.77	1.89	2.03	2.17	2.32	2.48
8.0	3.82	4.10	4.39	4.70	5.03	5.38	5.75	6.15	6.56	7.00	7.46
8.5	11.2	11.9	12.7	13.5	14.4	15.3	16.2	17.2	18.2	19.2	20.3

Figure 4-3: A Table for converting total ammonia to % free ammonia based on the aquarium temperature and pH.

parts per million (ppm): one part of compound in question in one million parts of solvent. This is equivalent to milligrams per liter ($^{mg}/_L$).

the free form. So, 2 *ppm* X 0.0189 = 0.04 *ppm* of free ammonia. This level is probably only minimally stressful to the aquarium inhabitants and is no immediate danger. Acceptable levels for ammonia are < 1.0 *ppm*, however ammonia should be undetectable if the biological filter (the nitrogen cycle) is functioning properly.

Find Related Information at: www.AquaChemPublishing.com

Correcting Ammonia Mayhem

Nature has created two easy to use remedies for ammonia removal in aquarium water. They are: 1) The Nitrogen Cycle, and 2) Zeolite Rock (see also **Chapter 3**).

The first remedy, as described previously, is the bacterial conversion of ammonia (NH_3) to nitrite ion (NO_2^{1-}), and eventually to nitrate ion (NO_3^{1-}). It's important to note that most aquatic plants absorb ammonia directly (as ammonium ion, NH_4^{1+}). Aquarists can take advantage of this fact to fairly quickly remove ammonia from their aquarium water. This short-circuiting of the nitrogen cycle will minimize the production of nitrite and nitrate that are further along in the process. If the latter part of the nitrogen cycle isn't well developed in this way, the death of a large plant or a large fish can produce extremely high levels of ammonia in a very short period of time that will be very slow to convert to nitrite (since there wasn't a large need for *Nitrosomonas* bacteria previously). If this happens, the ammonia must be reduced quickly to prevent toxicity.

The second remedy is the mechanical filtering of ammonia molecules out of the water by trapping them in the pores of the zeolite rock. Zeolite is a type of aluminosilicate clay that per chance happens to have just the right pore size to trap ammonia molecules. Zeolite chips can be regenerated by baking them in a 350°F oven for several hours. There are also synthetic molecular sieves that remove ammonia in exactly the same way and can be regenerated in the same way.

As mention in **Chapter 1**, unique aquarium products exist that can sequester ammonia almost instantly. The harmless reaction byproducts are then acted upon by the biological filter.

Find Related Information at: www.AquaChemPublishing.com

One of these products is chemically known as sodium hydroxymethanesulfonate and is sold by Kordon under the trade name AmQuel®. It's also sold by Tetra under the trade name AquaSafe®. This product is purported by its makers to remain active in the aquarium for ammonia scavenging unless removed by activated carbon or by water changes.

Another of these products is sold by Aquarium Pharmaceuticals under the trade name Ammo-Lock 2®. These products provide hobbyists with a fast and convenient way to eliminate the danger of ammonia in their aquarium water.

Testing Nitrites

The most common nitrite test kit is one that is based on the Griess Reaction, or a slightly modified version of it. With this type of kit, you place a known volume of aquarium water (usually 4-6 milliliters) in a clear test vial. Three to eight drops of an acidic sulfanilamide reagent is then added to the test vial. This is followed by the addition of three to eight drops of *N*-1-naphthylethylene-diamine dihydrochloride solution (NED for short). After ~5 minutes, the resulting color of the solution is compared to a color gradient nitrite chart to determine the concentration in either ***ppm***-NO_2^{1-} or ***ppm***-N(itrogen). Variants of these types of kits also exist in which the liquid indicator is replaced by a powdered, granular, or tablet form of indicator.

The Griess Reaction is what is called a diazotization reaction. In this type of reaction, an amine is converted to a diazonium salt with acidic (usually HCl is the acid) nitrite ion (NO_2^{1-}). The sulfanilamide reagent used in nitrite test kits has an

parts per million (ppm): one part of compound in question in one million parts of solvent. This is equivalent to milligrams per liter ($^{mg}/_L$).

Find Related Information at: www.AquaChemPublishing.com

amine group that is diazotized by whatever nitrite is present in your aquarium test water. The diazonium salt is then reacted with NED reagent to form a colored azo-dye that we can see. The more nitrite -- the more azo-dye -- and the darker the color.

Acceptable levels for nitrites are < 15.0 *ppm*. Again, if biological filtration (the nitrogen cycle) is functioning properly, nitrite levels should be almost undetectable.

Correcting Nitrite Mayhem

There are both naturally occurring and synthetic ion-exchange resins that will remove nitrite *ions* (NO_2^{1-}). The nitrite *ions* are usually replaced with chloride ions (Cl^{1-}), so there is no adverse affect on pH or *buffering capacity*. These ion-exchange resins don't work instantaneously and may require several days to make a noticeable change in nitrite levels. These materials can be regenerated by soaking them in a saturated sodium chloride (NaCl, table salt) solution.

ion: an atom that has gained or lost electrons and, as a result, is charged. i.e. NaCl (table salt) in water exists as Na^{1+} and Cl^{1-}.

buffering capacity: buffering is the resistance of water to a change in pH. Its capacity is based on the number of moles of acid or base required to effect a one unit change in pH.

While these "quick fixes" do exist for such a problem, it is a good idea to try to emulate nature and complete the nitrogen cycle naturally. I call them quick fixes because they work faster than the nitrogen cycle, and so they are relatively quick fixes.

Testing Nitrates

The most common nitrate test kit is one that uses cadmium metal to reduce the nitrate (NO_3^{1-}) to nitrite (NO_2^{1-}). The resulting nitrite can then be tested in a similar way to that described previously. With this type of kit, you place a known volume of aquarium water (usually 4-6 milliliters) in a clear test vial.

Find Related Information at: www.AquaChemPublishing.com

Chapter 4: *The Nitrogen Cycle*

Powdered cadmium metal and sulfanilamide (or sulfanilic acid) is then added to the test vial. This is followed by the addition of NED or some other reagent (sometimes gentisic acid) that will form an azo-dye. After ~5 minutes, the resulting color of the solution is compared to a color gradient nitrate chart to determine the concentration in either ***ppm***-NO_3^{1-} or ***ppm***-N(itrogen). Variants of these types of kits also exist in which the liquid indicator is replaced by a powdered, granular, or tablet form of indicator. Acceptable levels of nitrates are < 150.0 ***ppm***. Nitrates can increase with time if the nitrogen cycle is incomplete.

Correcting Nitrate Mayhem

There are both naturally occurring and synthetic ion-exchange resins that will remove nitrate ***ions*** (NO_3^{1-}). The nitrate ***ions*** are usually replaced with chloride ions (Cl^{1-}), so there is no adverse affect on pH or ***buffering capacity***. These ion-exchange resins don't work instantaneously and may require several days to make a noticeable change in nitrate levels. These materials can be regenerated by soaking them in a saturated sodium chloride (NaCl, table salt) solution.

Again, while these "quick fixes" do exist for such a problem, it is a good idea to try to emulate nature and complete the nitrogen cycle naturally.

A natural solution to elevated levels of nitrates is the use of one or more of a select few species of aquatic plants (i.e. Hornwort, see **Figure 4-4**) that can absorb the nitrate directly for conversion into plant proteins. As explained previously, nitrate is usually utilized by terrestrial based plants that live in or near the water and

ion: an atom that has gained or lost electrons and, as a result, is charged. i.e. NaCl (table salt) in water exists as Na^{1+} and Cl^{1-}.

buffering capacity: buffering is the resistance of water to a change in pH. Its capacity is based on the number of moles of acid or base required to effect a one unit change in pH.

Find Related Information at: www.AquaChemPublishing.com

most aquatic plants absorb ammonia directly (as ammonium ion, NH_4^{1+}).

Figure 4-4: A photograph of Hornwort (*Ceratophyllum demersum*), an easily grown free-floating surface plant that directly utilizes nitrate (NO_3^{1-}) as an energy source.

So an aquarist can either intercept the ammonia with a traditional aquatic plant before it is converted to nitrates, or they can utilize the nitrates once formed with one of the unique species of aquatic plants mentioned above. In either case, the nitrogen cycle is completed naturally with a minimum of human intervention.

Chapter 4: *The Nitrogen Cycle*

Chapter At-A-Glance

- The nitrogen cycle is nature's way of getting nitrogen (N_2 in chemistry shorthand) from one organism to another -- nitrogen recycling of sorts.

- fish take in nitrogen in the form of protein (containing amino acids) and excrete nitrogen in the form of ammonia. This ammonia is now available to other organisms as their nitrogen source.

- The Nitrogen Cycle
    - Ammonia (NH_3)
    - Nitrite (NO_2^{1-})
    - Nitrate (NO_3^{1-})

- Symptoms of a Broken Cycle.
    - If ammonia levels are high (> 2 ppm) and the aquarium is past its initial cycling - The "Break-In Cycle".
    - Remedy:
        - Remove ammonia immediately by:
            - performing a partial water change.
            - adding zeolite rock or synthetic molecular sieves to the filter medium.
            - Plant the aquarium with traditional aquatic plants that utilize ammonium ions (NH_4^{1+}) as there nitrogen source.
    - If nitrite levels are very high (> 15ppm and the aquarium is past its initial cycling - The "Break-In Cycle".

Find Related Information at: www.AquaChemPublishing.com

- Remedy:
    - Remove nitrites immediately by:
        - performing a partial water change.
        - adding naturally occurring or synthetic ion-exchange resins to the filter medium.
- The bacteria that are necessary for the nitrogen cycle may have been killed by some chemical additive or disease treatment. As long as nitrite levels are maintained at acceptable levels (> 15ppm) using the above methods, the bacteria will re-colonize and biological filtration will resume.

- If nitrate levels are very high (> 150 ppm).
- Remedy:
    - Remove nitrates immediately by:
        - performing a partial water change.
        - adding naturally occurring or synthetic ion-exchange resins to the filter medium.
        - Plant the aquarium with one of the select few species of aquatic plants that can utilize nitrates directly as their nitrogen source (i.e. Hornwort).

- Ammonia Testing:
- "wet" kit: done with 4 or 5 milliliters of aquarium water and color indicator.

Most common: Nessler's Reagent.

- "dry" kit: done with sample of aquarium water and dipping strip.

- Nitrite (NO_2^{1-}) Testing:
- "wet" kit: done with 4 or 5 milliliters of aquarium water and color indicator.

Most common: Griess Reaction.

- "dry" kit: done with sample of aquarium water and dipping strip.

Chapter 4: *The Nitrogen Cycle*

- Nitrate (NO_3^{1-}) Testing:

- "wet" kit: done with 4 or 5 milliliters of aquarium water and color indicator.
- "dry" kit: done with sample of aquarium water and dipping strip.

Neon Tetras (*Paracheirodon innesi*) are enjoyable egglaying community fish that are particularly beautiful in a larger group.

Red Eye Tetras (*Moenkhausia sanctefilomenae*) are another member of the egglaying Tetra family that are a good species for a community aquarium.

Find Related Information at: www.AquaChemPublishing.com

Elegant Angel Fish (*Pterophyllum scalare*) are nice egglaying fish for a community aquarium, but some more aggressive fish may nip their fins.

Bottom feeding Bronze Cory Catfish (*Corydoras aeneus*) are nice egglaying fish for a community aquarium.

Find Related Information at: www.AquaChemPublishing.com

Chapter 5: *Setup & Aquarium Maintenance*

Setup & Aquarium Maintenance

Probably the most difficult of all things to accomplish as a novice aquarist is the setup and maintenance of an aquarium. Even for a more advanced aquarist, it can be useful to have a place to record and track the important water parameters that should be checked regularly. This chapter will embody all of these necessities.

Initial Setup

When setting up your new aquarium, you must remember all of the factors that have been mentioned in previous chapters, as well as some new ones that will affect your success in the hobby. Some of these are: location, filtration, vegetation, and speciation. It is important to remember that most, if not all, of these items need to be considered relative to what species of fish will be kept in your aquarium. Because of this, this portion of this chapter will deal with a community aquarium (one that will contain docile and hardy fish that are tolerant of a variety of water conditions and can easily live together in harmony).

Location:

Put simply, do NOT place your aquarium too closely to a window. An aquarium is exposed to the environment on all sides. So it gains and loses heat very rapidly with the environment. An aquarium placed too near a window by an unaware aquarist can quickly overheat in the summertime from exposure to direct sunlight. That same aquarium in the wintertime will also become dangerously cold for tropical fish very quickly.

Another concern about your aquarium's proximity to a window is that of algae growth. The more sunlight that your aquarium receives, the heavier the algae growth will be. This is not necessarily bad in and of itself. However, if you intend to stock your aquarium with higher order plant-life, the algae will use up the nutrients that the other plants will need, making it very difficult to keep them alive. If you plan on stocking your aquarium with immortal plastic plants, you may actually want algae to grow in your aquarium. The algae can help maintain the nitrogen cycle as well as provide a source of food for fish with vegetarian tastes.

Filtration:

Once you've chosen the location for your aquarium, you must make the difficult decision of which type of filtration to employ in your aquarium. Some of the options are: a corner foam or box-filter, an undergravel filter, or an external filter. Each type of filtration has its own respective good and bad points, depending on your point of view. These points are summarized in brief in the following table. Each aquarist will have to determine for themselves if the points that are listed are either good or bad.

Chapter 5: *Setup & Aquarium Maintenance*

\multicolumn{3}{c}{**General Filter Parameters**}		

Filter Type	Power Source	Level of Maintenance
Box or Foam	Air Pump	High
Undergravel	Air Pump or Powerhead	Low
External	Motor-driven	Medium

As an example, corner foam or box filters remove particulate matter quite well, provide fairly good biological filtration, and have a low initial cost. These types of filters can clog frequently (especially the foam type), the replacement filter floss is rather costly for the box type, and biological filtration can be disrupted without <u>careful</u> "cleaning". These filters can require weekly maintenance in a heavily stocked aquarium, if not more frequently.

Undergravel filters remove particulate matter rather well, provide excellent biological filtration, and have a mid-level initial cost. The biological filtration can be adversely affected by disease treatments with obvious dire consequences. Some species of plants do not well tolerate the constant water flow around their root systems. These filters require infrequent maintenance, monthly at most.

External filters, of which there are many types, remove particulate matter VERY well, provide good to excellent biological filtration, and have a mid-level to high initial cost. These filters usually require weekly or biweekly maintenance.

Following this book's philosophy, it is recommended that you employ the type of filtration that most closely mimics nature. That type is <u>undergravel filtration</u>. Just as in nature, the particulate matter settles to the bottom and is filtered out by the gravel. Here it slowly decomposes and enters into the nitrogen cycle. The only major difference between undergravel filtration and nature is that you must vacuum your aquarium gravel periodically to prevent "clogging" of the biological filter.

Vegetation:

Following this book's philosophy, it is recommended that you stock your aquarium with higher-order plant-life. Novices should plant their aquaria with hardy, undemanding species of plants like: Corkscrew Vallisneria (*Vallisneria spiralis*), Crystalwort (*Riccia fluitans*), Hornwort (*Ceratophyllum demersum*), Java Moss (*Vesicularia dubyana*), Ribbon Wapato (*Sagittaria subulata*), or Water Primrose (*Ludwigia repens*). After the aquarium is well established and the novice is more experienced, other more demanding species of plants can be introduced.

NOTE: It's probably a good idea for novice aquarists to plant their aquaria after they are past the "break-in" or conditioning period. The reason for this suggestion is that the plants short-circuit the nitrogen cycle and actually lengthen the break-in cycle.

Speciation:

All of the previous topics are dependent upon this one, the choice of species of fish to keep in your aquarium. For example,

Chapter 5: *Setup & Aquarium Maintenance*

some species of fish (goldfish, cichlids, etc.) are constantly disturbing the aquarium gravel. If you intend to keep these types of fish, you will probably want to choose a filter other than the undergravel type and will want to plant your aquarium with hardy, free-floating plants that don't need a stable place for rooting. Most "community tank" species of fish are docile and won't have a drastic impact on the decisions needing to be made in the previous sections.

Conditioning an Aquarium

Conditioning an aquarium is quite simple if you have access to an established aquarium. Simply place a handful of gravel from the established aquarium in your new aquarium and the "Break-In", cycling, or conditioning period will be greatly shortened, if not eliminated. Unfortunately, most novice aquarists don't have such access. If you are one of the unlucky masses, don't despair, conditioning an aquarium is still very simple it just takes a lot longer and requires much more patience.

Step #1: Set up your aquarium following the outline described previously, taking into account, location and filtration. Add chlorine/chloramine-free water and begin filtration. Adjust the heater(s) to an acceptable temperature for the species you want to keep (for a "community tank" this is usually around 76°F or ~ 24°C). Test your aquarium water parameters: pH, GH, KH, and ammonia (nitrite and nitrate should be zero at this point). Adjust them, if necessary, to the levels required by the species of fish you want to keep. Allow the aquarium to equilibrate over night to ensure that the heater(s) is/are set correctly and that the water parameters remain constant. Record these initial water parameter values at the top of the "Conditioning Period Chart" on **page 70**.

Step #2: Check the water parameters (pH, GH, KH, and ammonia) once again before adding any fish. <u>Add 1 or 2 hardy fish for every ten gallons of aquarium volume.</u> Some good species of fish for this purpose are: simple guppies, small goldfish, or platies.

Step #3: Check pH and ammonia levels every day for 1 to 3 weeks. The ammonia level will begin to rise significantly near the two-week mark, unless the aquarium is planted. If the ammonia level gets above 1.25-1.5 ppm, perform small partial water changes (~ 10-15%) with "conditioned" water (same pH and chlorine/chloramine-free) each day until the ammonia level remains below 1.25 ppm. Be Patient! During this time, nitrite levels will begin to rise. Unless your aquarium is overstocked, this increase will not become a problem. To be safe, begin checking nitrite levels <u>every other day</u> beginning in the 2nd week. **Note:** The nitrite increase will be delayed if water changes were required for ammonia stress.

Chapter 5: *Setup & Aquarium Maintenance*

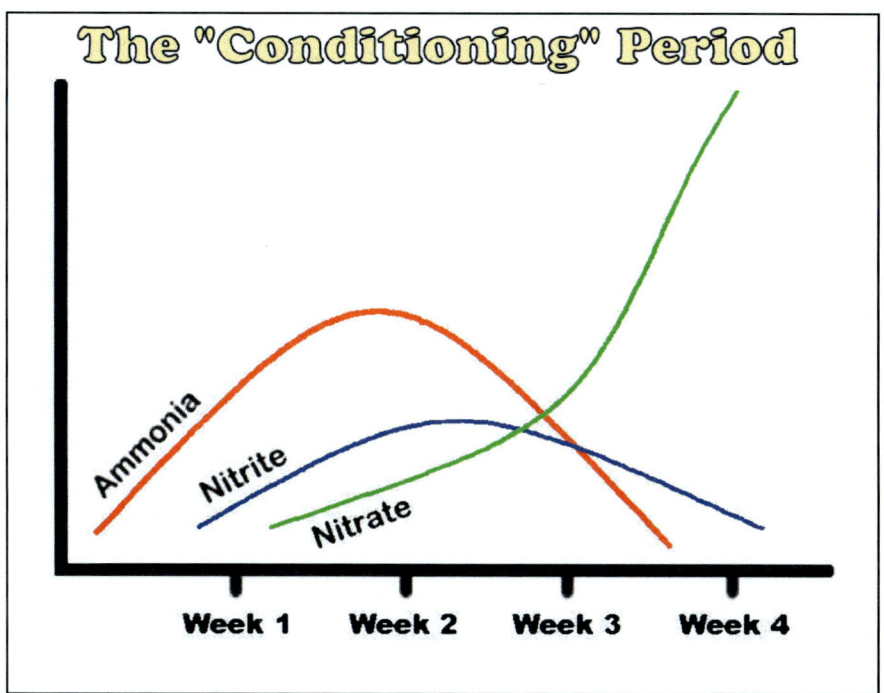

At this point, you are well on your way to a conditioned aquarium. Nitrite levels will begin to decrease and nitrate levels will begin to increase. Once nitrite levels again reach zero, your aquarium is "conditioned" or "cycled". This usually takes at least 4 weeks and can be up to 8 weeks or more depending on your aquarium conditions, so be patient! Test nitrate levels once a week beginning in the 4th week or after nitrite levels reach zero. At this point, you can adjust GH and KH to better suit the species of fish and plants that you intend to keep in your aquarium.

Step #4: Congratulations! You now have a conditioned aquarium and you can add less hardy species of fish, 1 or 2 each week, until you have a fully stocked aquarium. You can also add hardy plants, if desired, 1 or 2 each week, until you have a fully planted aquarium.

Find Related Information at: www.AquaChemPublishing.com

Conditioning Period Chart

Initial water parameter values for:

pH: _____ KH: _____ GH: _____ Ammonia: _____

	Sun	Mon	Tue	Wed	Thu	Fri	Sat
Week 1 pH NH_3							
Week 2 pH NH_3 Nitrite							
Week 3 pH NH_3 Nitrite							
Week 4 pH NH_3 Nitrite Nitrate							
Week 5 pH NH_3 Nitrite Nitrate							
Week 6 pH NH_3 Nitrite Nitrate							

Find Related Information at: www.AquaChemPublishing.com

Chapter 5: *Setup & Aquarium Maintenance*

Week 7 pH NH_3 Nitrite Nitrate							
Week 8 pH NH_3 Nitrite Nitrate							
Week 9 pH NH_3 Nitrite Nitrate							
Week 10 pH NH_3 Nitrite Nitrate							
Week 11 pH NH_3 Nitrite Nitrate							
Week 12 pH NH_3 Nitrite Nitrate							

Find Related Information at: www.AquaChemPublishing.com

Aquarium Maintenance

For any aquarist, it can be useful to have a place to record and track the important water parameters that should be checked regularly. Here are some suggested testing intervals for new aquarists.

Weekly	Biweekly	Monthly
pH	KH	GH
Ammonia	Nitrite	Nitrate

Once you become more familiar with your aquarium, you can better determine the frequency with which you need to test the water parameters.

Another important part of aquarium maintenance is that of water changes. Generally speaking, partial water changes of 10-15% should be performed about once a month. If your nitrogen cycle and other water chemistry is well balanced, this interval can be lengthened to bimonthly or slightly longer. As discussed previously in this book, there are a couple of options for what type of water to use for these partial water changes. **Option #1:** use "conditioned" tap water (approximately the same pH, GH, KH, etc.), or **Option #2:** use distilled water of the same pH as your aquarium water. Unless you have an extremely well balanced aquarium, that is, just the right amount of filtration, vegetation, speciation, etc., it's a good idea to follow Option #2. Undesirable compounds accumulate in an unbalanced aquarium over time, that is GH, KH, nitrate, etc. can all gradually rise over time. Many of these components are already in

Chapter 5: *Setup & Aquarium Maintenance*

tap water, so you're just contributing to this undesirable accumulation. In other words, you're negating some of the benefit from performing partial water changes. This is counterproductive and a waste of your valuable time. One caveat, though, do **NOT** use distilled water for larger water changes! A sudden fluctuation in water chemistry will cause undue stress on the inhabitants and can cause the untimely demise of more sensitive species.

One final suggestion, water changes are also a good time to "vacuum" the aquarium gravel. Most aquarium vacuums siphon water out of the aquarium to create the vacuum effect, so a sharp aquarist can kill two birds (vacuuming the aquarium gravel **and** removing 10-15% of the aquarium water) with one stone, so to speak.

Note: The tables on the next two pages are provided as useful guidelines for an aquarium maintenance schedule. Copies of them can be made so that you can have a running record of your aquarium water parameters in the event that a problem should arise.

Good luck & enjoy!

Harlequin Rasbora (*Trigonostigma heteromorpha*) are egg-laying fish that are well-suited for a community aquarium.

Find Related Information at: www.AquaChemPublishing.com

Monthly Maintenance Schedule

Month: _____

	Sun	Mon	Tue	Wed	Thu	Fri	Sat
Week 1 pH NH$_3$ KH Nitrite							
Week 2 pH NH$_3$ GH Nitrate							
Week 3 pH NH$_3$ KH Nitrite							
Week 4 pH NH$_3$ Vacuum & Water Change							

Find Related Information at: www.AquaChemPublishing.com

Chapter 5: *Setup & Aquarium Maintenance*

Monthly Maintenance Schedule

Month: _____

	Sun	Mon	Tue	Wed	Thu	Fri	Sat
Week 1 pH NH$_3$ KH Nitrite							
Week 2 pH NH$_3$ GH Nitrate							
Week 3 pH NH$_3$ KH Nitrite							
Week 4 pH NH$_3$ Vacuum & Water Change							

Find Related Information at: www.AquaChemPublishing.com

Index

A

acid, *8, 18, 22, 23, 25, 26, 28, 29, 31, 34, 39, 42, 44, 45, 46, 47, 48, 58, 59*
aerator, *5*
alkaline, *12, 18, 21, 33, 39, 42, 44, 55*
alkalinity, *18, 33, 39, 42*
ammonia, *8, 10, 11, 12, 15, 21, 23, 31, 33, 49, 50, 51, 52, 54, 55, 56, 57, 60, 61, 69, 70*
ammonium ion, *51, 55, 56, 60*
analog, *2*
anions, *11, 36*
aquarium heater, *6, 15*
aquarium heaters, *5, 6*
Aquarium Maintenance, *74*

B

biological filtration, *51*
bleach, *8*
box filters, *67*
break-in cycle, *68*
Break-In Cycle, *52*
brine shrimp, *50*
bromothymol blue indicator, *25*
buffering capacity, *18, 22, 23, 24, 26, 32, 33, 34, 39, 41, 46, 47, 48, 58, 59*

C

calcium, *11, 23, 36, 39, 40, 41, 45, 48*
calcium carbonate, *36*
calcium chloride, *37, 39*
calmagite, *45*
carbonate, *11, 18, 21, 23, 24, 28, 33, 36, 37, 38, 39, 40, 41, 42, 44, 46, 48*
carbonate **equilibria**, *21*
carbonate hardness, *39, 42, 44, 46*
Carbonate Hardness, *38*
cations, *11, 36, 38*
chloramine, *7, 8, 10, 11, 12, 15, 69, 70*
chlorine, *7, 8, 9, 10, 12, 15, 69, 70*
Conditioning an Aquarium, *69*
Conditioning Period, *70, 72*
Corkscrew, *68*

D

dechlorinate, *9*
dechlorinating, *9*
Dechlorination, *9*
de-ionized water, *45, 46*
Denitrification, *18*
DH unit, *35*
diazonium salt, *58*
distilled, *12, 13, 15, 45, 46, 47, 48, 74*
distilled water, *12, 13, 15, 46, 47, 74*

E

EDTA, *44, 45, 48*
electronegativities, *1*
equilibria, *18, 21, 27, 28, 30, 41*
equilibrium, *8, 18, 26, 27, 40, 41*

F

Filtration, *66*
free ammonia, *55*

G

GDH, *35*
general hardness, *44*
General Hardness, *38*
gentisic acid, *59*
GH, *37, 38, 44, 45, 48, 69, 70, 71, 72, 74, 76, 77*
Griess Reaction, *57, 58, 62*

H

heat capacity, *5, 15*
Hornwort, *53, 60, 62, 68*
hydrogen bonding, *2, 4*
hypochlorite, *7, 9, 10*

I

ion, *3*
ionic, *3, 26*
ions, *3, 7, 12, 18, 20, 26, 28, 29, 41, 44, 45, 46, 48, 58, 59, 61*

Find Related Information at: www.AquaChemPublishing.com

K

KH, *38, 39, 44, 46, 48, 69, 70, 71, 72, 74, 76, 77*

M

magnesium, *11, 36, 39, 40, 44, 45, 48*
magnesium carbonate, *36*
magnesium sulfate, *36, 39*
molarity, *19*
molecular sieves, *10, 56, 61*
moles, *19*
monobasic sodium phosphate, *20, 24, 29, 31, 32, 34*

N

NED, *57*
New Tank Syndrome, *52, 53*
nitrate, *11, 21, 36, 51, 52, 54, 56, 59, 60, 62, 69, 71, 74*
nitrite, *51, 52, 56, 57, 58, 59, 61, 62, 69, 70, 71*
Nitrobacter, *51*
nitrogen cycle, *10, 18, 49, 50, 51, 52, 54, 55, 56, 58, 59, 60, 61, 62, 66, 68, 74*
Nitrosomonas, *51*
<u>Non-Carbonate Hardness</u>, *39*
non-KH, *39*

P

parts per million, *7, 35, 55*
Permanent Hardness, *39*
pH, *iv, 5, 12, 17, 18, 20, 21, 22, 23, 24, 25, 26, 28, 29, 31, 32, 33, 34, 39, 41, 42, 44, 45, 46, 47, 48, 54, 55, 58, 59, 69, 70, 72, 73, 74, 76, 77*
pK_a, *27, 28, 29, 42*
ppm, *8, 9, 10, 35, 54, 59*

R

reverse osmosis, *12*

S

sodium bicarbonate, *20, 22, 28, 32, 33, 34*
sodium dihydrogen phosphate, *29*
soft water, *23, 24, 28, 29, 33, 46*
Softening Hard Water, *45*
sulfanilamide, *57, 58, 59*
Sulfate Hardness, *39*

T

thiosulfate, *9, 10, 15*
titration, *45, 48*
tubifex worms, *50*

U

undergravel filter, *66*

V

Vallisneria, *68*
Vegetation, *68*

W

water change, *10, 13, 24, 28, 29, 33, 45, 46, 61, 62*
water hardness, *12, 35, 36, 37, 38, 39, 40, 42, 46*
water parameter, *70, 72*
Water Primrose, *68*

Z

zeolite rock, *46, 48, 56, 61*

Find Related Information at: www.AquaChemPublishing.com

Made in the USA
Coppell, TX
03 June 2022